LIFE ETERNAL

Also by Martin Israel and published by SPCK

Living Alone
The Inward Journey to Fellowship (1982)

The Pearl of Great Price
A Journey to the Kingdom (1988)

Night Thoughts (1990)

LIFE ETERNAL

Martin Israel

First published in Great Britain 1993
Society for Promoting Christian Knowledge
Holy Trinity Church
Marylebone Road
London NW1 4DU

British Library Cataloguing-in-Publication Data
A catalogue record for this book is available from the
British Library

ISBN 0-281-04684-0

Typeset by Pioneer Associates, Perthshire, Scotland
Printed in Great Britain by
Biddles Ltd, Guildford and Kings Lynn

My thanks are due to my old friend Leslie Price who has put so many pieces of information at my disposal in the writing of this book. I asked for his help, knowing how learned he is about the entire parapsychological field, but what he has produced transcended my fondest hopes.

Contents

Preface

Death is still a great taboo subject among many people. They are certainly interested in the process of dying now that hospices have captured public imagination as places where one can die in proper personal dignity. Bereavement too has become of wider interest with the development of counselling services. More succour is available for those who are left behind after a loved one has died. But what happens to those who have made the great transition? The agnostic tends to deny the very possibility of personal survival after the body dies, a hard point of view that is being supported by a growing number of Christians despite the credal basis of their faith. This agnosticism is to be respected, since truth should not be concealed behind impressive religious language. Some scientists attempt to explain life itself on a mechanistic basis. How can there be any meaningful existence of a person once the brain is dead? Here we come to the perennial philosophical argument about the relationship between brain and mind, between body and soul. Mere academic debate soon reaches an impasse; we require data outside the scope of materialistic science, valuable as this is in its own sphere of operation.

In this book I have marshalled the data of parapsychology, or psychical research, in order to support the view that brain and mind, body and soul, are in fact two separate categories of personality, marvellously linked while we are alive on this earth, but capable of various degrees of detachment under circumstances of bodily injury, and also in some people who are in good physical and mental health. I have little doubt that the data of authenticated communication between the dead and the living as collected and scrupulously analysed by specialists in parapsychology cannot simply be swept under a carpet of worldly scepticism. They are worthy of study at least as components of the human personality, which may well transcend mere flesh and blood. Parapsychology strives for a scientific status, but its data are sporadic and rarely open to the reproducibility that material scientific research demands. Nevertheless, these data are too familiar to be dismissed out of hand either as wishful thinking or sheer fraud perpetrated on a gullible public by accomplished magicians.

The subject is not made easier by the prohibitions against psychic exploration contained in the Bible. Thus, while the up-to-date liberally-minded Christian is liable to dismiss parapsychology as flawed thinking, the more earnest believer sees the workings of demonic forces in all phenomena that might point to the survival of an aspect of the personality after its physical body has perished. In this account of life eternal I commence with vigorous earthly existence and the process of ageing, and then proceed to the event of death from both a physical and a psychical point of view. The fascinating near-death experience indicates that the two are less irreconcilable than sceptics would have us believe. Then follows the more controversial matter of spontaneous communication from the dead to the living. This may be direct, or through irreproachable mediumship, or following the memory of a past life on earth. After this I consider the Christian theological basis for a belief in an after-life, and how informed parapsychological studies can help in substantiating that belief. Belief admittedly rests on a basis of faith, but a real faith need not fear the meeting with knowledge. Only then does what we believe become attuned to the age in which we live, no longer resting on ways of thinking that seem archaic and barely comprehensible among scientifically educated people.

Eternal life is, however, much more than survival of the personality after the death of the body, important as this is as an interim process. Eternal life is a state of personal growth into the fullness of being, seen in Christian terms as the person of Christ himself. Such growth cannot be attained in the course of a single life on earth even among the greatest of the world's saints. Indeed, how such people have been able to maintain this sanctity during their lives is a mystery when we consider the low state of morality of human institutions in general.

I hope that this book may help the Christian believer enunciate the final sentence of the Nicene Creed during the Eucharist with the joy of corporate conviction:

We look for the resurrection of the dead
and the life of the world to come. Amen.

Martin Israel
November 1992

Our attitude to all men would be Christian if we regarded them as though they were dying, and determined our relationship to them in the light of death, both of their death and of our own. A person who is dying calls forth a special kind of feeling. Our attitude to him is at once softened and lifted on to a higher plane. We then can feel compassion for people whom we did not love. But every man is dying, I too am dying and must never forget about death.

> Nikolay Alexandrovich Berdyaev, from
> *The Destiny of Man*

Worrying about immortality is for people of rank, and especially ladies, who have nothing to do. But an able man, who has something regular to do here, and must toil and struggle to produce day by day, leaves the future world to itself, and is active and useful in this.

> Goethe, from Eckermann's *Conversations*

Christ likes us to prefer truth to him because, before being Christ, he is truth. If one turns aside from him to go towards the truth, one will not go far before falling into his arms.

> Simone Weil, from *Waiting on God*

LIFE

*When I look up at your heavens, the work of
your fingers,
at the moon and the stars you have set in place,
what is a frail mortal, that you should be
mindful of him,
a human being, that you should take notice of him?*

Psalm 8.3-4

CHAPTER 1

The Gift of Life

He was made as we are that he might make us what he is himself.

The glory of God is a living man; and the life of man consists in beholding God.

Both of these quotations come from the text of *Against Heresies* by St Irenaeus. They remind us of the privilege of having been born human, and of how precious our life on earth is. When I meditate on these two sentences my mind dwells on the lives of two people whom I knew well and who are now dead.

The first was a splendid young doctor. He came of a distinguished line in his profession and attained high honours, both at school and at the university where he trained for his profession. His postgraduate life was a round of successes, justly deserved but severely deprecated by some of his peers who sneered at his career advancement as being due to his contacts on the higher rungs of the medical ladder; his father had been knighted for his services to medicine. When I started my own lecturing work his wife, an erstwhile speech therapist, put me in contact with someone who was a great help to me in voice production, and so launched me on the work I was to do as medical lecturer and later as a preacher and retreat conductor. My friend died precipitately when a bomb intended for someone else exploded under his motor car as he started up the engine one morning to drive to work. He died apparently meaninglessly as a victim of a terrorist outrage, and was buried with high honours. His death was as successful as was his life, for material honours had not

corrupted him or led him to despise anyone less
fortunate than he was. It was his deprecators who were
left exposed in their meanness. In a small way he had
shown something of the way of his Lord, Jesus Christ.

The second person who comes to mind was also a
doctor. His lineage was far less splendid than that of
the other man, but what he lacked in social dignity, he
possessed in resourcefulness. He made his way to the
top rung of his profession, and was powerful both in
medical politics and in controlling his juniors' lives. To
get on well they needed his testimony, a situation
common in most of the 'higher' professions, and he
made demands on their time, compelling their cooperation in his private work. At home, too, he was a
tyrant. His wife died fairly young of cancer, and his two
sons, though educated at leading schools, failed to
enter university and drifted into a drug-taking sub-
culture from which they were eventually rescued by
devoted Christian evangelists. At his death many fine
things were said in the obituary columns of the medical
and general press, but no one mourned his departure;
fortunately from his point of view he died just as he
was about to retire from his hospital work. His life
story forces us back immediately to Jesus' burning
question: 'What does anyone gain by winning the whole
world at the cost of his life? What can he give to buy his
life back?' (Mark 8.36-7). The life Jesus is speaking of
is the integrity of a person's true being, or soul.
Whatever integrity this individual ever had was
sacrificed on the altars of false gods: money, power and
social position. While my first friend adorned these
worldly attractions by his humility and love, the second
made a terrible parody of them. The things of the world
need not be despised, but they are not to be coveted.
They are here for our learning in the school of life; as
servants they are invaluable, but as masters they are
destructive.

'Remember your Creator in the days of your youth, before the bad times come and the years draw near when you will say, "I have no pleasure in them"' (Eccles. 12.1). These solemn words remind us of the ongoing flow of life and its end in disease and ageing. The moment that gives us life also presages its ending. In the midst of life we are in death; we are all proceeding onwards towards the august moment of our eventual transition. If we are wise, we accept its intimations with gratitude, and if we are sensible we also prepare for it now. Life and death are part of a continuous process, a mysterious journey into the unknown which paradoxically is part of our very being. Death is the instant when the mortal body is shed and a new consciousness assumes control. Death strikes unpredictably; it may be at the peak of youth, following an accident or the stark inroads of a mortal disease. It may crown a busy life before, or soon after, the fruits of retirement can be enjoyed. Or it may signal the end of a worn, senile, decrepit body that has striven to keep alive for as long as possible while the soul longs for release to move onwards to the experience of new realms of understanding. Sometimes it is a newly born baby who makes the unheralded transition, or a child too innocent to have experienced anything of the creative ecstasy of life or the disillusionment of dashed expectations and human betrayal. The mystery of death is also the mystery of life, a mystery which is beyond the scope of the unaided intellect but which is being unveiled before us each moment. If we are aware, we can know this unveiling, but if we are caught up in our private affairs to the exclusion of the greater whole, we remain ignorant.

All too often we miss the splendour of the present moment through anxious, often fruitless, speculations about the future or regrets about a past that cannot be altered. When we consider the dictum of St Irenaeus, quoted at the head of this chapter, that God's glory is a living person, and the life of the human person consists in beholding God, we can see how often we fall below the standard set before us. The human person has an animal body but is endued with spiritual apprehension: when he or she attains a degree of self-knowledge, the intuition rises above the earth to the heavens where a glimpse of meaning can be divined amid the noise and distractions of the world in which our life has to be conducted. To be aware of the heavenly realm, to which death is the portal of entry, we do not have so much to think about spiritual things as to be fully aware of the present situation. If we cannot find God's works in the world around us, we are unlikely to come to know him in spiritual exercises carried out privately. On the contrary, it is when we have given ourselves completely to the world in the form of the particular work in which we are engaged, that we are able to be fully receptive to the love of God, both at that moment and also during periods of quietness when our consciousness can ascend without sensory interference to the heavenly realm. As we give of ourselves, so we receive; but any self-centred action merely separates us from the desired one. When, however, we lose ourselves in service, God shows himself as divine purpose that speeds us on our way with inner rejoicing. He is indeed the way, the truth and the life, shown definitively in the ministry of Christ up to his death and resurrection. And as St Irenaeus reminds us, he was made human so that he can make us into something of what he is – but in our own bodies and with our own special character traits.

The gift of life is primarily the gift of our own unique essence. Self-esteem is the basis of a life well lived. As with so much else on the spiritual plane, the psychology of the self is based on a paradox. If we do not love ourselves, we will not be able to love anyone else; those whom we believe we love will turn out to be mere figments of our own desire for support and confirmation. We cannot relate in truth with others until we can relate in love and gratitude to ourselves. This is impossible for the unaided human consciousness, especially when we see the imperfections that appear to lie at the very root of our personalities. But when we know the stillness of the present scene, we give God a chance to make himself known to us, to enter our inner being as Jesus entered the homes of the many sinful people who invited him to eat with them. And as Jesus flowed out in love to these people, so God pours out his healing grace to all who will let him enter. This is an action of pure faith, of simple trust, such as a small child would make. We are healed, not by our own actions but by the power of God working within us. When we have experienced the divine presence deep within us, our lives are transformed by love. We cease to be concerned about the effect we are making on other people, and instead we flow out quite spontaneously in recognition and love to everyone. 'We love because he loved us first' (1 John 4.19) states the position excellently. Once we know this love, we cannot but esteem ourselves properly, and by extension esteem others likewise. And so the second great commandment, to love our neighbour as ourselves, is fulfilled by the first one, to love God absolutely, with a love that reciprocates God's prior love of everything he has made, including our own unworthy selves.

A person who loves himself or herself takes the self for granted as the daily round of work is performed. A person with a shaky self-esteem tends to arm themselves with external attributes, such as social contacts, academic degrees or political power, as much to impress the self as other people. Self-esteem degenerates into pride when we cannot accept the gifts of others. This is in itself, paradoxically, a manifestation of a shaky esteem of ourselves. To esteem ourselves properly is to

esteem other people equally, even those of low degree or
criminal tendency – but for God's grace we might have
been in their position; but to whom much is given, of
that person much is expected. The Pharisee in the
parable of Luke 18.9-14 could never have understood
this point of view unless he too were to fall foul of
fortune and descend to the depths experienced by the
squalid tax-gatherer. (In all probability this occupation
had been thrust upon the tax-collector through difficult
circumstances, and then his will to good was insidiously
seduced by the money he obtained in the course of his
traitorous work for the Roman authorities.)

To live properly is therefore to act from a centre of
will that can rise free from the conditioning of the past
or the demands of the present. This freedom is a
function of the soul, and until we know our own soul we
cannot be free to do the work which we were born to
perform. We are, of course, products of our past and
workers in the present; we are not meant to abdicate
our worldly responsibilities. But if we function from our
true being, we will do our accustomed work efficiently
and in harmony with others. Our emotions will no
longer dominate our thoughts and actions but will
rather play their part in the total performance of our
lives. When we live properly, it is the soul that directs
us, while the intellect and emotions are antennae that
guide us in purposeful action minute by minute. The
conscious self that we know is the ego; when we are
living as we ought to, the ego reflects the soul. But, as
we know only too well, the ego tends to identify itself
with the desires and the passions of the world. St Paul
movingly describes this conflict between the lower
nature of sin and the higher nature of the image of God
within us all in Romans 7.14-25: only the presence of
Christ can rescue us from a body doomed to death. This
presence is known to us both within our soul and as the

historical figure who assumed the sin of the world so as
to redeem it from death to resurrection.

These things cease to be mere psychological dogmas
when we consider our life on earth and what is in store
for us. Success in the world's eyes is attaining the fruits
of one's activities in such realms as the learned
professions, finance, politics, the arts and sciences, or
the more modest but far more basic sphere of family
life. To rise to the summit of the professional ladder
makes one an object of general esteem. Yet all gifts and
talents, the attributes by which a person is valued by
society, are subject to attrition when that person retires
from active work and is obliged to confront the far
greater test of the life within. While we are at the peak
of our powers we can take shelter behind our works and
the body by which they are performed. It can easily
happen that an apparently laudable show of good works
hides a selfish private life, if not one that wreaks havoc
on those in close contact with us. Those around us may
be temporarily deceived; but much more serious is the
self-deception that allows us to evade the truth of the
situation. As St Paul writes, 'Make no mistake about
this: God is not to be fooled; everyone reaps what he
sows. If he sows in the field of his unspiritual nature, he
will reap from it a harvest of corruption; but if he sows
in the field of the Spirit, he will reap from it a harvest of
eternal life' (Gal. 6.7-8). If we transpose this fundamental law of cause and effect into the events of life, we
can see that the individual who has evaded the duties
and responsibilities required by society, and through
society to the wider creation, inevitably falls back into
an isolated existence dominated by an ageing body. 'He
gave little and so received little in return'; this would be
a stinging judgement on such a life. In our youth we
may appear to be independent of the help of other
people, but when we grow old our eyes are opened more

widely to our impotence as isolated individuals. This is
the 'diminishment' described by Teilhard de Chardin.

Human life (and probably the life of our animal
cousins) is above all a series of relationships. We grow
into the adult state by the friction against, no less than
the friendly support of, those with whom we live and
work. The friction wears away the selfish edges of our
personality, while the support strengthens us in the
hour of our distress and arms us for the trials that lie
ahead. We in our turn play our part in the social and
spiritual development of those around us. It may be
fondly hoped that when social justice has been attained,
a finer person will emerge; but history shows us how
self-centred and predatory human nature so often
remains, even in times of plenty. If people knew the
glory of their lineage, that they are made in something
of the divine nature, they would cease to scramble for
personal honours and would instead give themselves in
joy to serve their fellows. This service is an act of pure
love: accepting individuals as they are and then being
able to direct them to become what they were meant to
be, children of God. It is God's love that is the directing
power; when we love we cease to try to influence affairs
on our own, but are instead obedient to a wisdom far
beyond our own understanding.

In fact, people as individuals are often remarkably
kind and considerate. It is when they come together as
discrete groups, united by a particular interest that
separates them from their fellows – be it religious,
professional, cultural, or national – that their individual
identity tends to be supplanted by a common resolve or
dedication that makes them a threat to those around
them. This is indeed the test of personal integrity, to
work conscientiously and with loyalty in one's particular
setting, while never letting the contours of the divine
image within be blurred, or even obliterated, by
considerations of expediency or material gain. This is a

hard demand to make on our poor human nature, heir to so many afflictions both innate and environmental; but how we grapple with them determines our state in the life beyond death.

Our consideration so far has dealt exclusively with those of us who are born into comfortable families with able bodies and minds and a definite, if mutable, aim in life. When we consider the millions of starving people in the world, with no tangible future ahead of them apart from their terrible deprivation, we may wonder what gift God has given to them apart from their emaciated bodies. It is said that the dignity of some of these people is a lesson in itself; most have a religious culture to support them, but their travail is beyond belief. Yet they too have a lesson to learn and a contribution to bring to the consciousness of those who are in better circumstances. The same applies to people who are born with severely deformed bodies or defective brains. We begin to learn slowly in the school of life that there is more to a person than the physical body, vital as it is for any independent existence. There is more to life than meets the casual eye, a theme that assumes increasing relevance as we consider the process of ageing.

CHAPTER 2

The Gift of Age

No spring, nor summer beauty hath such grace,
As I have seen in one autumnal face.

These lines from the ninth of John Donne's Elegies, entitled 'The Autumnal', tell of a life well spent. We owe our existence to God's grace, to his unconditional love by which all creation is sustained and our own infinitely smaller lives are supported in the devious channels we so frequently traverse before, like the Prodigal Son, we see the light and start to do what is required of us. And then the divine grace pours upon us like an inexhaustible stream of love. We, in turn, reflect that grace upon all whom we meet, so that they are lifted out of their usual prison of private thoughts and negative emotions - 'What are we to eat? What are we to drink? What shall we wear?' (Matt. 6.31) - and feel something of the love of God far beyond anything they might articulate. Some people exude that grace even when young; it is not to be confused with charm, which can be manipulated and is evidently mutable even when sincere. Grace is an inner blessing; it comes from God and we are its servants. It lubricates the machinery of common life in the form of considerate deeds towards other people, and if we live in conscious awareness of the wants of others, grace informs our actions as it civilizes our attitudes.

Even if we were not conspicuously gracious when we were young and healthy, the experience of life will deepen our sympathies as we too partake of some of the heartbreak that punctuates mortal life. Our expectations have not been fulfilled, our family life may have been saddened by death, or by the unredeemed loss of a child who has insisted in going its own way while its capabilities have been left unused. I often think of the father of the Prodigal Son, whose love forbade him to interfere with the stupid boy's headstrong action in taking his money and leaving home to live a life of riotous excess. This love was as great as that with which he received his destitute son home again (Luke 15.11-32). The outer manifestation of that love was the father's gracious attitude which boiled over into joyful exultation when his son, who had been as good as dead, suddenly turned up from nowhere. There was no question of the father cross-questioning his son or demanding better behaviour in future. His grace flowed out to the young man, who was surely converted to God's love and started to live a useful life on the paternal estate.

We start to make our old age in our youth; if we were concerned about the welfare of other people when we were young, that concern will show itself in our faces and general demeanour when we are of advanced years. We will demand attention as little as possible, always thinking of the feelings of others before our own. This is the essence of sensitivity to other people's needs - not intruding and pushing our opinions and proffered assistance on to them, but rather waiting for a tacit request before acting. Many eager proselytizers of various faiths and political attitudes thrust their wares in the faces of their fellows so insistently that they evoke an immediate negative reaction. A person of grace respects the feelings and attitudes of others, showing a courtesy that is the foundation of a sound relationship which may in time mature to a warm friendship. The important thing is never to hurry or precipitate a formal decision according to one's own judgement. The experience of a well-tested adult life brings with it this grace, and a wise elderly person has something precious to offer.

When does a person become old? Our age is in fact a product of our own mind - we are as old as we think we are. This dictum is excellent as far as it goes, provided we are sensible enough to respect the inevitable slowing up of certain bodily and mental processes with the passage of time. There are a few landmarks that leave their impression: the age of forty signals the middle years, while that of sixty heralds the elderly period, marked also by the status of senior citizens, a little later for men than for women. The menopause reminds the woman that one vital function, that of childbearing, is now at an end. It should also cause her to reflect on the other themes of life and death. The man, on the other hand, has no clear signal of receding youth, and can live at a boisterous level for some decades, until mortal disease suddenly strikes. Nowadays the span of human life in the developed countries has lengthened so considerably that anyone dying before the age of seventy is regarded as young by some people. In fact, the older we become, the further distant do we place the portal of old age. At present this would be set by many at eighty years, but there are numerous octogenarians who are helping their juniors admirably. I personally have had invaluable assistance in spiritual matters from women well over ninety years old; our collaboration has brought renewed strength to both of us. It is a good practice to keep our bodies and minds always in a state of function. Our minds most need matters of constant interest to prevent them from regressing into vacancy. In the same way a well-exercised body is kept in the finest trim. Illnesses modify this dictum, of course, but even then it is good to exercise the body and mind for sheer enjoyment.

The great gift of age is experience - experience of

people, of circumstances, of personal humiliation, of forgiveness and growth, of the things of this world and of their gradual relinquishment. When we were at the height of our powers, we almost identified with those powers and the work by which they were actualized in the world. As those powers decline, and our directive role in society is relinquished, we are left increasingly to ourselves: the present scene continues without us, or at the most we are elected emeritus members of our professional group. But there is a larger scene in front of us – our own inner nature and the life which it creates for our deeper education. It may be 'a terrifying thing to fall into the hands of the living God' (Heb. 10.31), but the terror of a personal void which was once filled by outer activities and self-inflating ventures can be of suicidal intensity. The person who has filled their life by working with concern and caring for others while still flourishing in youth and middle age, will find a harvest of good will to greet them as retirement closes a chapter of activity in a well-spent life. As we have already remarked, we make our old age in our youth; and if that earlier period has already been adorned with loving care, a foundation of inestimable value has been established on which to construct an edifice of personal enjoyment and spiritual growth.

'Men must endure their going hence, even as their coming hither: ripeness is all,' says Shakespeare in *King Lear*. The end of life is that ripeness which can fill all who meet such a person with delicate pleasure and deeper thanksgiving. What has matured within, like the fruit of a tree, is now available to others: the quality is wisdom, the synthesis of worldly knowledge and a broad experience of life made profound by our openness to God. We may recall Job's words when he has lost everything of personal value: 'Naked I came from the womb, naked I shall return whence I came. The Lord gives and the Lord takes away; blessed be the name of

the Lord' (Job 1.21). All that is left is what we have
built up during the course of our active life; it was all
that Job had left to sustain him during his terrible
ordeal which was to culminate in a direct vision of God.
We, too, need to be divested of personal conceit if we
are to be open to the full presence of God. The
experience may be hard to bear, but the fruit is a
renewed personality of which it can be said, 'I have
been crucified with Christ: the life I now live is not my
life, but the life which Christ lives in me' (Gal. 2.20).
There is no striving for personal achievement, since in
the light of reality the things of this world are seen to
be tools whereby we may grow in experience but which
are left behind when our work is completed. This is the
meaning of retirement; it falls on all who have attained
the requisite age, and the hope is that they have reaped
a rich harvest of wisdom from their efforts. Then they
may leave the practical work to those who are to follow
while they enjoy the fruits of their deeper labour in
reflective silence.

Is there any useful work for a retired person to do,
apart from serving on committees, going back to fill a
locum post, or taking charge of the grandchildren so as
to give their parents a time for rest and recreation?
There is indeed some work which is essential for the
spiritual growth of the person: developing an awareness
of the present situation, both in the immediate vicinity
and in the wider world. This awareness should prove
itself in action, by helping locally according to one's
capacity and by the more interior work of prayer.
Theoretically retired people should have much time for
prayer, since they now have less to distract their
attention. In fact, praying in an emotional void can be
more difficult than when we are balanced precariously
on a knife-edge of family commitment and even of
personal survival. The stress of such a dynamic
situation can afford a very real stimulus for prayer that

may be absent when all around is secure. To the outsider, a religious community might appear to offer an ideal place for prayer, inasmuch as its way of life would seem to ensure material tranquillity, but in fact even the most contemplative of orders is active in looking after the house and preparing meals, to say nothing of caring for the property that so impresses visitors. This, in addition to the inevitable friction between individuals, creates an atmosphere of stress that heightens the life of prayer which is the great contribution of such communities generally to the spiritual well-being of the world.

In other words, prayer is often most effectual where there is a degree of distraction; it seems that our relationship with God may be strongest when we have to pay due attention to the world, even to the point of relinquishing our inner peace for a time. When we become more experienced in the way of prayer, times of silence and of activity flow together into a single stream of loving obedience to God and service to our fellows. If the ageing person has grasped this sequence of prayer earlier on in life, the capacity for silent communion will be a point of growth and also a great gift to those in the vicinity. There will certainly be little time for loneliness.

A great gift which comes with age is the opportunity to be oneself. The demands of the world have been negotiated, and now we can settle down into ourselves, taking stock of the lessons that the past has taught us about our attitudes. We can now examine emotions, especially such adverse ones as anger, resentment, bitterness and wounded self-esteem, in the security of retirement from the world's critical judgement. Our essential work is to know ourselves as we really are, using the gospel criterion, 'Where your treasure is, there will your heart be also' (Matt. 6.21). When we were young and unthinking, our treasure may well have been the things of this world, like money, prestige, social eminence or professional glory; but with the advent of retirement these things fall increasingly into the background, as they will do finally when we die. What is left is ourself, devoid of any worldly power but full of our own personality, with which we are to make the great transition when the physical body is left behind and a new life opens up for us. The things of this world are not to be dismissed simply as futility, as in the view of the writer of Ecclesiastes (1.2); on the contrary, they are essential means of spiritual growth so long as we are active participants in the world's councils. But if we cling on to them they become our idols, and eventually our prisons also; whereas if we are wise enough to take their essence into our lives, they become tools of priceless value. And when we are finished with them, they are left inviolate for the use of a younger generation. They are indeed our final will and testament, even at this present moment, which could, at least theoretically, be our last one on earth. The person who is full of his or her integrity will not depend on outer attributes or possessions for self-affirmation; instead these can be used for the benefit of others whom the person serves.

Our great gift to the world is ourself: we are each unique, and when, in the love of God, we can come to terms with our various defects, even these are of inestimable help in the life of the community. What we all have in common is suffering. By contrast, our various gifts tend to separate us, and only when we have acquired the humility that comes from debasement do these play their full integrating role in our relationships with other people. We may remember with profit the Lord's answer to St Paul when the thorn in his flesh was not removed despite his thrice-repeated plea for healing: 'My grace is all you need; power is most fully seen in weakness' (2 Cor. 12.9). If Paul had been delivered from his impediment, whatever it may have been, he might all too easily have slid into an attitude of righteous judgement on all those who remained unhealed despite the ministrations of their fellow-Christians. To know ourselves in the trough of despair is the fruit of deeper experience. To bring that knowledge into our intercourse with the world is a very great healing achievement, first for ourself and then for those around us.

The ageing process is one both of joy and of menace: joy at retirement from active work with its strains and responsibilities, menace at the awareness of leaner years to come when the body's functions will be less efficient and the mind may focus less sharply. All this may take place many years hence, and so it is right to enjoy the gift of age here and now. The years immediately following retirement are often especially pleasant. We are still well enough to enjoy the natural scene and to travel to distant places. We have the time to read the books which previously lay unopened because of the demands of work. We are able to listen with quiet enjoyment to music that comes to the world as God's gift through the inspiration of great composers and interpreted in love by performers who have lived that gift in their own lives. We can even enjoy ourself more modestly in our own music-making, or painting; what we lack in sheer genius we may attain in satisfying ourselves and giving pleasure to those around us. We do not have to strive for an excellence that is clearly beyond us, but can simply revel in our own capacity.

This brings us to a final consideration. Most people are not endowed with genius; their lives will appear uninspiring when they compare themselves with other people. They have not attained the rank or standing that they wanted in their imagination, and by comparison with the celebrities they are mere nonentities. As we grow older, these judgements become less significant. What really matters is how we have lived our lives in relation to our own special talents, responsibilities and defects. These are the tools which we brought into life with us, and we use them in every circumstance that our own existence meets. We reveal ourselves most clearly in our attitudes to mundane events, in the Good Samaritan type of situation (Luke 10.29-37). This is much more important for our own spiritual growth than many professional triumphs, even when we are hailed as masters by many people. The heart knows the truth, and it will not be deceived by earthly show which, like the writer of Ecclesiastes, it will know to be futility masquerading as success. As we grow old the scales fall from our eyes, perhaps in a rather less dramatic way than they did from Saul of Tarsus when Ananias laid his hands on him after his encounter with Jesus on the road to Damascus (Acts 9.18), but nevertheless no less definitively. We see the weakness underlying all shows of strength, the fallibility of all who were considered experts in their subject, and the nobility of the little ones who were able to give up their very lives for the love of someone dear to them. 'When the evening of this life comes, we shall be judged on love,' writes St John of the Cross. The widow's mite was more highly esteemed than the larger donations given by the wealthy worshippers to the temple treasury (Mark 12.42-4).

DEATH

---

*Remember your Creator before the silver cord is
snapped and the golden bowl is broken, before
the pitcher is shattered at the spring and
the wheel broken at the well, before the dust
returns to the earth as it began and the
spirit returns to God who gave it.*

Ecclesiastes 12.6-7

CHAPTER 3

Death: A Meditation

'In the midst of life we are in death.' This death is more than the cessation of bodily activity that we all call death, and which may befall any of us, even at this moment. Even more cogently, it is the end of a present phase of awareness, with the promise of a new venture into the unknown.

Who am I? If I identify myself with my body of flesh and bone, I will soon come to see that there is little of this that can be called permanent. The cells of my skin, as they reach the surface, die and are shed. The cells of my inner organs undergo cycles of growth, maturation, senescence and death, and are in turn replaced by new cells. There are some cells which cannot be replaced: the neurones, or nerve cells, of my brain undergo death throughout my adult life and are not replenished. Even my bones, which superficially seem hard and durable, are undergoing constant remodelling; old bone is slowly removed and new bone is laid down in the lines of stress where support is most immediately necessary. The young person I was many years ago is barely recognizable as the older adult I now am; and in due course, if my life is preserved, I will present the shrunken, stunted body of an aged individual. Everything about my physical body is in a state of constant disintegration and replacement. As I grow older, so the replacement becomes less perfect, until I can no longer survive the attacks of hostile agencies from outside and invidious assaults from within.

Nor is my mental and emotional life any less dynamic. When I was a child my horizons were to a large extent limited by thoughts of school and passing examinations.

When I was adolescent I left school and enjoyed a phase of higher education. Soon the memory of school life faded away, and I was fully occupied as an undergraduate. In due course I qualified in my work and entered the larger, more unprotected world to practise it. Very soon my life at training college had passed into the half-lights of distant memories. At present I am still well occupied with my work, but I am also thinking about the time of retirement – where I will go then, and how I will be accommodated when I am aged and infirm, always assuming I am not called away before then. But be that as it may, one thing is certain: at a moment in time I will be finally and decisively called away from my present concerns and activities, and will have to make my peace with a new world of which I know very little. This is the meaning of death as seen from my point of vantage: the entrance into a new realm of existence, glimpsed by faith rather than illuminated by prior knowledge.

When I was a child I spoke, thought, and reasoned like a child (1 Cor. 13.11), but when I grew up into an adult I parted with childish concepts and put on the mind of a questing person. The dreams, fantasies and illusions of my childhood are now distant memories, while I have grown in sympathy and understanding for many people whom I would previously have disregarded because of the prejudiced atmosphere in which I was reared. Growing into life is also a growing towards death, which is the great leveller. But this levelling effect is merely a surface phenomenon: the outer dross of personality is worn down, but the core within us all, the pearl of great price that is our true self, the soul, shines radiantly when the outer layers of debris are removed.

It becomes clearer as I get on in years that the real purpose of my evanescent life on earth is to help me to grow into a better integrated person; so that when I have finally to quit the flesh I will have a well-formed personality, based on wise mental attitudes and moral responsibility, with which to carry on my conscious life into the formless world beyond the grave. Everything I have in this world is in a state of flux, and nothing outside the central core of my identity, my soul, is truly my own. I am growing into this wisdom through the education wrought by life's vicissitudes, especially the wounding and self-revealing relationships with other people I repeatedly have to undergo. The way of transcending selfishness to attain the full glory of the inner Christ (that 'point' of the soul where God is known, and often called the spirit), is by loving service to my fellow creatures. This service has no attachment; it does not cling nor demand recognition. When there is non-attachment there is a perfect freedom in the depth of the relationship. Death, in its many guises, is here to teach me the meaning of non-attachment, for when I am about to die I will attain detachment from even my most precious belongings, which I can even now see to have an existence apart from my own selfish use of them.

As I progress in the spiritual life I become less attached to past regrets and future hopes and fears. My mind rests on the moment in hand, and distracting thoughts cease to be intrusive. Eventually I learn to live entirely in a single moment in time, and I discover in the consciousness of this moment the point of my identity. When, through the journey of experience, I know this fact of existence, I have moved from the life of imprisonment in matter to the life of eternal freedom. Then I am ready to face my death with composure, knowing that my work on earth is done.

CHAPTER 4

Preparation for Death

Since none of us knows the time of our death, it follows that we all should be prepared in the present moment, both materially and spiritually, for our end. In fact, we tend to avert our gaze from this ultimate event until circumstances draw us ineluctably to its threshold.

To 'put out affairs in order' is a common figure of speech for making our will, something that should be done at least as soon as we have responsibilities to those around us. This will may be altered on a number of occasions as our family situation becomes more complex, since our first priority is to our immediate family and close circle of friends. By contrast, we should make any outside bequest according to our personal preference, based on an informed knowledge of the charity in question. Most of us have our own favourite charities, but it is a good rule to investigate their financial status before automatically donating future funds. The most honourable charitable concerns send out an annual balance statement to their subscribers. The point of this discussion is to stress that money is an important commodity and should be handled carefully and responsibly; merely disposing of it profligately can be as reprehensible as spending it entirely on personal pleasure.

Far more important, however, is our spiritual stock-taking, which should proceed day by day, preferably before we retire each night. We should spend a little time recollecting the day's events, with sorrow at our failings mixed with joy at the divine pardon. The pleasant events of the day should cause us to rejoice as we thank God for the many gifts that lighten our labours as we journey from darkness to light. The point of the matter is to remember God constantly in the daily round; then alone will his presence be close during times of trial. This is the meaning of St Paul's injunction to 'pray without ceasing' (1 Thess. 5.17). If our silent prayer life is proficient, we shall be able to depend on it when, like Jesus in Gethsemane, we are in sore straits. This is a deeper application of Joseph's advice to Pharaoh to hoard sustenance during the profitable years, so that we may have ample supply to fall back on when disaster strikes (Gen. 41.33-6). We, in our childish ways, forget the times of plenty in our agitation when disaster strikes.

Just as we must bequeath our material possessions to those who follow us, so we should groom our juniors to continue the work we have started, or inherited as part of our seniority. To be able to stand back and allow a younger person to wield their own authority is a sign of a mature awareness; one is reminded of the words of John the Baptist with regard to the blossoming genius of Jesus: 'He must grow greater; I must become less' (John 3.30). Such an attitude is a product of disinterested love: of care given quite selflessly to the one who follows, until we can say, with Simeon, *Nunc dimittis* (Luke 2.29-32), closing a chapter of our life in peace. Even in our emancipated era there are still many aged parents who exert a tyrannical emotional blackmail over their children. If they were properly educated in the work of living, they would be able to relinquish this sorry control and live in quiet contentment in the present moment. The care of aged parents is a matter of mounting concern as people generally live longer than in previous generations; but it is the rule that pleasant people will find ready help when they become incapacitated, whereas those whose lives were selfish when they were active will find a barrier of antagonism when they need constant assistance. This is because they manifest an unpleasant air of complaint tinged with ingratitude, no matter what is done to please them.

The ego is an essential part of the personality; as a servant it is admirable, but once it takes control it becomes a ravening beast that will let nothing alone. A sound preparation for death involves the civilization of the ego so that it becomes the window of the soul: the words of Jesus quoted in St Mark's Gospel, that 'whoever wants to save his life will lose it, but whoever loses his life for my sake and for the gospel's will save it' (Mark 8.35), contrast the ego (psychical) life which must perish at death with the soul (spiritual) life which continues after the body dies. In the fully realized person the ego and the soul coincide, so that such a person can say in the words of Galatians 2.20: 'I have been crucified with Christ; the life I now live is not my life, but the life which Christ lives in me.' Such a state of consciousness is rare in the round of the day's work, but it is the prerequisite for any truly caring relationship.

A problem that confronts all ageing people is to know when to yield independent existence and settle in a residence where their needs are taken care of but their private life is severely restricted. It is important to retain one's independence for as long as possible; a good compromise is sheltered accommodation where a person lives in a community of fairly healthy old people, has a separate, fully self-contained flat, but with a warden in residence, in close contact with each tenant and available to provide assistance in a situation of emergency or sudden illness. Such accommodation does not usually have nursing facilities, but these can be easily arranged should the necessity arise. When a person is severely disabled, there can be no question of much independence, and a residential home becomes necessary. The probability must be faced that the most desirable accommodation may not be available when it is needed. It is advisable to apply for residence some time before the final move becomes inevitable, and then to accept a place when it is offered; a severely handicapped applicant might later be unacceptable, whereas previously he or she would have been welcomed as a relatively able-bodied member of the community, and eligible for nursing care when the physical or mental condition required it. It is wise to spend a few weeks in such a home to see how one fits in with the general atmosphere before the final, decisive break with past spaciousness and freedom of activity is made, and one enters an unknown community with strangers, some of whom may show the ravages of senility. It may be necessary to try a number of residences before the most suitable is found. Such discrimination is far from ungracious, for the home will probably be one's last on earth.

This rather bleak consideration is lightened by the calm simplicity of advancing years; we find that many of the possessions we needed earlier now become amazingly irrelevant to our present position. Just as the expansive domain of a family house condenses into the compact space of a small flat once the children have left home, or bereavement has sadly ended a loving earthly relationship, so the transition from this smaller space to the single room that is usually provided in residential homes for the elderly is often pleasantly smooth. Residents are usually called on to furnish the room, so that at least some of one's treasured possessions remain as a reminder of younger, more adventurous days. As we grow older a new awareness comes upon us, especially if defective hearing and sight deprive us of the precise appreciation of music and visual art. What on the surface seems a tragic loss can also be an entrance into an undiscovered world of inner feeling and remembrance, which I believe we shall explore much more finely in the life ahead of us when the failing body finally dies.

It is in human relationships that we approach the essence of our life, and what lies revealed is a clear testimony to the integrity of that life as well as an indication of how we may respond to the challenge of the future. With the ageing process we are brought solidly to confront the bitter toll of relationships broken either through our own self-centred carelessness, or the shallowness of those whom we confidently believed were friends but whose interests were elsewhere when we needed their support most. My mind inevitably goes back to Jesus' three disciples, Peter, James and John, who were unable to stay awake with him even for one hour during his mortal struggle with the concerted forces of evil that so often dominate our world (Mark 14.37). Later, they were ignominiously to run away from him altogether when he was betrayed into the hands of sinners, thereby saving their own lives and also showing the futility of what those lives represented (Mark 14.50). Our own past history, and that of our friends and associates, mirrors these events, albeit in small compass, though often we are so insensitive to the deeper issues of relationships that we remain blissfully unaware of what we are doing. We may, for instance, suddenly give vent to inherited prejudice of race, class, or religion, sometimes quite spontaneously without reference to an outside precipitating situation, and cause grave offence to another person. That the offence was unpremeditated is of small consolation to the one whose self-esteem has been hurt; and indeed it was the prejudice that was the focus of sin, whether or not it was openly articulated. All such attitudes will ultimately be brought to light, whether now or in the life beyond death; and so a wise person takes note of his or her inner reactions as soon as possible. We have already emphasized the value of recollectedness at the end of each day in this respect.

A personal affront may be hard to forgive until our inner sight is deflected to the many times when we ourselves have behaved inconsiderately to other people.

It is therefore important that forgiveness should inspire our present attitudes and actions; in this way the apparently destructive process of the future can be halted and reversed. On the whole it is the introvert, whose awareness is directed inwardly, who has greater difficulty in forgiving others than the extrovert, who looks more happily outwards into the surrounding world. But a spontaneous extrovert forgiving and forgetting can simply indicate a shallowness of the emotions and an insensitivity to the feelings of other people, so the one psychological type is neither better nor worse than the other.

In the end, it is what we make with the various traits with which we have been endowed that determines our success in the larger life that far transcends anything our little world can comprehend. And yet not the slightest movement we make goes unheeded, for every action bears its own consequences both now and in eternity – in fact both states are one, the world we inhabit being essentially a place of experimentation and of the actualization of our gifts. We should remember that a defect may be more useful to us in this world than many assets, which can so easily separate us from other people, and give us a sense of superiority that proves an illusion when we too are called on to stand up and be counted for the values which we affirm with the mind. 'What does anyone gain by winning the whole world at the cost of his life?' We considered this question earlier, and it is at the heart of any preparation for death, when the ego life will indeed be at an end.

If we are to know the way forward in trust and love, it is worth while considering the dynamics of forgiveness. The first truth is that in ourselves we are not able to forgive anyone, not even ourselves. When the scribes were affronted by the forgiveness proclaimed by Jesus to a paralytic, they were, theologically, quite right: God alone can forgive sins. They did not, however, know the identity of the man who had pronounced forgiveness (Mark 2.1-12). God's nature is always to have mercy, to seek a reconciliation with his children; as St Paul put it, 'God was in Christ reconciling the world to himself' (2 Cor. 5.19). Since forgiveness comes from on high, if we want to be forgiven and to forgive those who have hurt us (the two processes are inseparable), we must lift up our consciousness to God in simple prayer. This prayer is a pure act of self-giving, rather like the prayer the tax-collector made to God in the parable (Luke 18.9-14). If the desire is heartfelt, it will be granted, even if some time may elapse before we are aware of the change in our consciousness, a change signalled by a warming of the heart and a relaxation of the whole body. A person's sense of humour, previously frozen, can now melt into a smile of satisfaction and even boil over into a peal of laughter as the folly of the past is seen so clearly. Anyone with a keen sense of humour must be struck by the enormous incongruity of the human situation and the reality of life: the serious posturing of the human in face of this greater reality causes an intellectual tension that is relieved when we suddenly see the situation in all its absurd futility in the perspective of the vastness of creation. We no longer cling to any affectation, but simply let go in the delight of inspired ignorance. It need hardly be said that anyone who takes themselves too seriously in respect of a system of belief, whether religious or secular, lacks a sense of humour; their intensity sees little alternative to their way forward and they are likely to regard any view contrary to their own as treason. Many converts to a religious faith or a political party may have a long journey to undertake before their eyes are opened to the uncertainty of any human institution, whether ecclesiastical or secular. As a person grows older the wisdom of humour becomes a bulwark in a life where everything is uncertain except the present moment. This is indeed one of the treasures of growing old, for we no longer need to stand with bated breath before the celebrities: all of us are on the same path, and God alone knows our situation and destination.

What I am saying is this: the proof of God's forgiveness is first of all a capacity to confront ourselves as we are, to smile at our infirmities, and to forgive ourselves without condition, in much the same way as the tax-collector was forgiven by God. We can then begin to love ourselves as we are; true love accepts the defects as fully as the assets. Thus Jesus shows the marks of his passion to his disciples in one of the resurrection appearances, and the absent Thomas will not be satisfied until he too has seen them (John 20.19-28). The wounds remain, but now as a basis of worship, no longer mere signs of humiliation. Once we can relax in the knowledge of our own worth, proved by God's acceptance of us, and filled with the unreserved love of God, our very being bubbles over in little streams of joy that flow to those around us, including the people who once injured us in word or deed. Nothing seems to matter any more in the indescribably glorious love of God. That we have all sinned and are deprived of the divine glory (Rom. 3.23), is somehow compensated for by the knowledge of God's intimate love for all his creatures, a love that ensures their eventual participation in that glory.

Prayer is an inscrutable activity; the more we try, the less we succeed, at least in terms of fulfilment of our petitions. This is because the ego gets in the way, knowing quite definitely what it wants but not having the patience to listen to a higher wisdom. Jesus promises, 'Ask, and you will receive; seek, and you will find; knock, and the door will be opened to you. For everyone who asks receives, those who seek find, and to those who knock, the door will be opened' (Matt. 7.7-8).

In fact the prayer is its own answer, but we must wait
in patience for its fulfilment in our lives, because until
we are ready we cannot use it properly. (This, incidentally, is why instantaneous healings at church services
or charismatic gatherings may not always be the
blessing one would expect: the person is best left to
assimilate a gradual improvement in his or her own
time so that caution and wisdom may govern life in the
future.) To pray for forgiveness is to be forgiven, but
the price demanded is to want to forgive others also. As
we are forgiven, so we worship in the love of God, and
bring everyone in with us in that worship. Forgiveness
attains its fulfilment when we can say, 'It doesn't
matter.' Then the cause of the conflict can really be set
aside and forgotten. Healing, including healing of the
unconscious mind, is then complete. The healed person
is stronger, more mature, and so the trouble is unlikely
to recur; and if it were to do so, the person would be
able to react in a much more adult, spiritual way of
rapid forgiveness. This forgiveness is very different
from the type of pardon that comes from personal
superiority, when the injured person looks down on the
offender, excusing the offence in terms of the offender's
background or mental instability. In true forgiveness
the offended stands alongside the offender, knowing
that a closeness of sin binds both together. Only God's
grace can effect a healing.

We should certainly seek a reconciliation with those
whom we dislike whenever possible. We must remember
Jesus' admonition, 'If someone sues you, come to terms
with him promptly while you are both on your way to
court; otherwise he may hand you over to the judge,
and the judge to the officer, and you will be thrown into
jail. Truly I tell you: once you are there you will not be
let out until you have paid the last penny' (Matt.
5.25-6). The journey to court can be compared with our
movement towards death where we shall have to face a

stern, but correct, judgement for the course of our life on earth. But in that judgement we too are part of the jury. The more we can put right here, the less the pain on the other side of death. This may involve a candid admission of guilt and a humble plea for pardon. We may be able to repair a past misdemeanour, just as we might hope that an injury committed against us may be equally compensated. Often, however, the wounded party is now dead; nothing we can do will reverse the wrong we did as far as that person is concerned. In this circumstance the way to make effective amends is to behave with charity to our neighbours who live alongside us. As Jesus put it, 'Anything you did for one of my brothers here, however insignificant, you did for me' (Matt. 25.40). We may rest assured that our wronged adversary is now a wiser person, and approves of our solicitude to a fellow creature. This, incidentally, is the defence against the accusation of partiality in intercessory prayer: we cannot name every person in the world individually, but if we pray in devotion for even a small sample, the power of that prayer radiates to many others who are not directly included.

It also needs to be said that our efforts at reconciliation should be guided by honesty. There are some people who are so entrenched in their own invariable rectitude that any thought that they also might be at fault is quite impossible for them to accept, let alone tolerate. Such people should be left alone until a deeper awareness of their own intractability comes to them. Love may indeed be the greatest of all the virtues, but it remains incomplete until the demands of truth have been satisfied. We may be sure that after the festivities given to celebrate the Prodigal Son's return home, he had to take a common place in the running of the estate. There he had to endure the company of his older, morally impeccable brother, whose very attitude would show his disapproval even if he were polite enough not to give voice to his sentiments. Only long effort by the erstwhile prodigal in their mutual interest would soften the hard shell of disapproval; and this is not entirely unreasonable. Forgiveness must be immediate, but then we have to start to put right some of the things we did imperfectly. In fact, the love that is the foundation of forgiveness so pours out of the one who is forgiven that he or she quite spontaneously proceeds to make generous amends for any past misdemeanour. It is in this way that faith is brought to life, for, as St James writes, 'Faith, if it does not lead to action, is by itself a lifeless thing' (James 2.17). To forgive does not entail making oneself a doormat to be walked over by all and sundry. Such an attitude in `effect denies a meaningful personal relationship in that one avoids a direct communication with other people. It can also have unpleasant masochistic undertones.

The person who is preparing for death ought to be more alive than ever. The mind should be active and alert as new interests, especially in intellectual and spiritual matters, take the place of a receding mundane view of reality. How fortunate are those who have already acquired wider interests while still at the peak of their career, whether that of a thriving professional person or a mother set about with husband and growing children in a fine home! In the Hindu scheme of spiritual life, the aspirant proceeds from the stage of student to that of householder, which ends at the birth of his grandchildren. He then retires into the depths of the forest, either alone or with his wife, where he proceeds to contemplate the great things of existence. The final stage is one of complete renunciation, perhaps at a holy place, where death is awaited in profound meditation. But it is important to note that God, however the Deity may be conceived, is the centre of this four-fold scheme of life. He is with the youth in his studies no less than in the arduous work of the husband or the contemplation

of the mendicant. The spiritual preparation for death
does not consist in investigating psychical matters
relevant to the question of personal survival of death –
while these are not to be dismissed out of hand, they
are essentially research tools for parapsychologists in
their quest for greater understanding of the human
personality, whether here or in a vaster canvas beyond
death. It is the more profound realities of the great
mystical tradition of the world that should guide the
thoughts of all who are moving towards the final point
of earthly existence. The centre of mystical awareness
is love; love alone prevails when everything else has
been withered by the pitiless inroads of time, decay and
death. Carl Jung's oft-quoted observation that amongst
his older patients there was no case of psychological ill-
health that was not ultimately related to a search for a
deeper religious meaning to life (*Collected Works* XI,
para 509), is crucial to our preparation for death. Only
as we ponder the deep things of God will we come to the
core of our own immortality.

This chapter has obviously been geared to the needs
of older people, because most of us, at least in the
developed countries of the world, will probably die in
our seventies or eighties. But death can also face a
younger generation afflicted with cancer or AIDS, or
the victims of accidents. Much of what I have been
recommending is apposite to young people also,
especially the thoughts about forgiveness and spiritual
living in the present moment. In Boswell's *Life of
Johnson*, he records Samuel Johnson as saying, 'Depend
upon it, Sir, when a man knows he is to be hanged in a
fortnight, it concentrates his mind wonderfully.' Fortunately, capital punishment is now banished from the
legal system in most of the developed countries, but
death can still meet us at any time. Therefore we should
all practise 'the sacrament of the present moment', as
the great eighteenth-century Jesuit spiritual director

J. P. de Caussade termed it in his masterpiece, *Self Abandonment to the Divine Providence*. In the present moment God is fully with us, but we, alas, are not with him, any more than the three disciples were with Jesus when they accompanied him to Gethsemane. They were there in their bodies, but their minds were elsewhere. In the present moment Christ celebrates the eternal Eucharist, and if we are with him moment by moment we will not lose anything of his body and his blood. 'The practice of the presence of God', the title of another masterpiece by the seventeenth-century Carmelite known as Brother Lawrence, is the way of preparation for death from the moment of our birth. Of course this becomes feasible only when we have grown into some sort of spiritual awareness, but to know God at all times is the purpose and end of our life, for in him we are eternally renewed.

CHAPTER 5

Dying:
The Renunciation of the Body

The drama of dying is our final renunciation of all the things of this earth. We have had our fill of the various joys and pains of existence and are now ready, whether heavy-hearted or with gratitude, to take our leave of them. Of course, our departure goes ahead whether we acquiesce or not; but if we have learned to prepare beforehand, we will have grown in wisdom with our life span and will be able to cooperate with the forces and powers that determine our spell in this world and lead us to our immediate destination: 'Now, Lord, you are releasing your servant in peace, according to your promise. For I have seen with my own eyes the deliverance you have made . . .' (Luke 2.29-30). Admittedly, none of us have seen this deliverance as clearly as did Simeon beholding the infant Christ; but those people who have lived constructively with society and in harmony with their deeper consciousness should be able to divine, albeit dimly, within themselves and in the final summing-up of their experiences, some pattern and meaning to their earthly existence, which sheds light on their destiny, and indeed on the destiny of all creatures.

Most of us are still like little children; at a certain hour those who look after us put away our toys and carry us protesting to our beds where we almost at once fall into the sound sleep of childhood, only to awake the next day refreshed and renewed to enter into further adventures. Nevertheless, the process of being separated from our earthly belongings is not pleasant when we grow into adult estate, because we readily fall victim to the misapprehension that we really own these things, instead of seeing ourselves merely as their custodians. Stewardship is an important experience for making us value the things of the world, but the good steward is always ready to hand back the material to the owner, who is God. If we have carried on our work well, more will be given us, but nothing is ours in perpetuity. We have no possession other than the focus of identity which we know as the soul or the spiritual self. In the enterprise of earthly life everything else drops away from us except the experiences derived from our stewardship. These add their quota to the soul's memory and the wisdom it accumulates for what is to follow in the time of our decline and the new life ahead of us afterwards.

To some, death comes suddenly, as after an accident or following the dramatic failure of an immediately vital organ. Others pass away painlessly in their sleep without having had any prior foreboding of their imminent dissolution. But most of us will experience the slow inroads of mortality, and will have to learn to make peace with the evanescence of earthly life. 'Naked I came from the womb, naked I shall return whence I came.' This is the heart of the matter: we must return, as we came, with nothing except ourselves, trusting that we have gained a little in psychological stature and spiritual understanding through the experience of incarnation. First we have to renounce our work, accepting that we shall never return to it. Then we dispose of our motor car, we quit our pleasant residence for a more modest abode, until one room - indeed one bed - is enough for us. We dispose legally of all our worldly possessions, and make our last communication with acquaintances, friends, and finally close relatives. Soon we are fighting for mortal life itself and our whole awareness is concentrated on this titanic struggle. We have finally to make our greatest earthly renunciation, that of the physical body.

It is on this facing of imminent death that we should now focus our attention. Most people would agree, whether or not they accept the possibility of an after-life, that it is the process of dying that is the most forbidding aspect of death. No matter how spiritual our outlook, we cannot evade our mortal anchorage in the physical body we inherit, and we are exquisitely sensitive to its pain and dysfunction. In some disease processes, for instance heart trouble, the end is seldom clear-cut; life may terminate with dramatic suddenness, and yet quite often it is prolonged for many years, with variable degrees of incapacitation. In the degenerative diseases of the nervous system, such as the common stroke and the tragic multiple sclerosis which tends to start in early adult life, existence may continue for a considerable time with all degrees of disability, ranging from complete helplessness to only slight weakness - and indeed spontaneous remissions may occur in multiple sclerosis even on some occasions when the patient seems beyond all human help; occasionally these remissions may last for so long that hope is held out for permanent recovery. Another very ominous nervous disorder is Alzheimer's disease, a slowly progressive degeneration of the brain in which there is increasing intellectual enfeeblement, so that finally the person may apparently not recognize even spouse and children. The distress this condition produces in the friends who once communicated normally with the sufferer may not be reciprocated in the patient, but what is going on in the deeper recesses of the mind we do not know. All this becomes relevant to any consideration of the life of the personality beyond the death of the body. It is a well-recognized fact that apparently unconscious patients may hear some of the conversation around them, including comments about their own state, which they may later repeat when their condition improves; therefore one should not discuss the condition of an unconscious person any more than one would that of fully aware patients in their hearing. Conversely, it is worthwhile speaking to an unconscious friend in hospital even though there can be no tangible response.

It is the inexorable progress of cancer that causes the most dread; the very word can send shivers down the spine until one has adapted oneself to its presence within one's body. It is often not appreciated that cancer can sometimes kill with comparatively little discomfort, and that its course is not invariably as relentless as is generally assumed. The occasional case of inoperable cancer may live on for a considerable number of years with only mild discomfort, perhaps succumbing to some other disease. It is well recognized that some types of widespread cancer may disappear even without treatment. These 'spontaneous remissions' are rare, and they cannot at present be explained satisfactorily on a purely scientific basis. Their very existence, however, reminds us of the uncertainty of all human predictions about the course and termination of disease processes. The claims of spiritual healers must also be interpreted in the light of the inscrutable course of many chronic diseases.

A very important development in medical practice in recent years has been the recognition that the slowly dying person is something more than a mortally diseased body to be helped on its way with graded doses of pain-killers. The advent of death is a most important experience ahead of us all, one in which the whole panorama of our life can be surveyed, and a final spiritual acceptance given both to what has happened in the past and to what we may encounter in the future. To facilitate this final appraisal the body should be in as comfortable a state as is possible. An illness may produce severe physical distress in its later stages - this distress may be predominantly pain, but there may also be breathlessness, cough and digestive symptoms. The object of treatment is to abolish all pain without significantly altering the patient's state of consciousness, so that he or she can communicate freely with the world with mental clarity. A fairly new medical speciality has been established to deal with this matter: it is known as palliative medicine, and its existence reflects the concern now accorded to the experience of death and what we, who are still alive and in health, may learn from it. Death is a junctional experience which touches medical practice, bereavement counselling, parapsychology, philosophy and theology. Even those practitioners who claim a complete atheism and a disbelief in the possibility of personal survival after bodily death are as deeply involved in this palliative medical practice as those who profess a religious faith. The development of palliative medicine began in separate medical institutions which were called hospices, but nowadays small units for the treatment of the dying are to be found in some general hospitals also. This seems right, inasmuch as the dying should be able to communicate their insights to those around them, albeit on an intuitive, psychical basis. The concept of terminal care includes all the procedures and ways of management that we have been considering.

To visit a hospice is often a radiantly beautiful spiritual encounter. Some of the patients were admitted in a state of severe physical distress, mental depression (the effect of a tacit rejection by their medical attendants and their family as being incurable and therefore a burden on all concerned), and spiritual confusion. They are welcomed by caring people, placed in pleasant surroundings, and treated as individuals once more. The regime of palliation of distress allows the dying patient to blossom into a fully authentic person, able perhaps for the first time in his or her life to face the ultimate facts of existence and to move towards the next stage in the courage of total awareness. Dying in such surroundings, while hardly a pleasurable experience, can nevertheless become a really creative one. While religion is never forced on the patient, he or she is enveloped in a community of caring people who, more by their demeanour and actions than by their words, reveal something of the presence of the eternal Christ who is incarnate in the bodies of all who do his healing work in the world, irrespective of their theological position. At present these terminal care units merely skim the surface of an ocean of human suffering, but they point the way forward to the time when all who care for the sick and dying will be imbued with a vision of life and death that proceeds beyond dissolution to survival and resurrection.

The physical process of dying can be harrowing, possibly more so to the onlooker than to the patient. Sometimes the end is unexpectedly rapid, but more often there is a gradual failure of bodily function until the person lapses into unconsciousness. Sometimes he or she may still be able to respond to conversation by gripping the hand of the person at the bedside, always a reassuring gesture. And then the coma becomes absolute; there is no further tangible response, the breathing may be punctuated by episodic hiccupping, which may be followed by the rather distressing 'death rattle', distressing to the onlooker rather than to the one who is dying. This noise is due to the obstruction of breathing by phlegm, or mucus, in the air passages, in addition to which the lungs may start to become water-logged, or oedematous, as the action of the heart fails. When the actual time of death draws near, the apparent struggle of the body to keep alive, the so-called death agony, seems to yield to a composure that is wonderful to behold. It calls to mind the so-called sixth word of Christ on the cross, 'It is accomplished' (John 19.30). 'Brother ass', as St Francis called his own body, has done its work and is prepared to yield its elements once more into the earth from which it was fashioned. If the person who is dying has used that body in edifying grace earlier on, something august seems to emanate from it as it dies. There is indeed an awesome beauty surrounding the body of a good person; it is that person's first memorial. One feels that the centurion saw this in the body of the crucified Christ: 'This man must have been a son of God' (Mark 15.39). It must also be said that the type of individual who has lived on a purely sensual level, with little concern about the welfare of anyone else, shows a less radiant body after death. Deeper consideration of this observation casts a shaft of light upon the important, though mysterious, doctrine of the resurrection of the body that is an article of the Apostles' Creed.

There is, I believe, an innate fear of death in all of us, no matter how strenuously we may, in our present moment of strength and apparent health, deny it. This innate fear is to our advantage, and that of our species, for without it we would tend to endanger our lives recklessly and so fall victim to accidents and infectious diseases. Many of the laws contained in the Pentateuch (the first five books of the Bible) have an emphasis on public health; the legislation against lepers - their affliction does not seem to have been modern leprosy but some other lesser infectious skin disease - and the prohibition against eating the flesh of pigs, which may harbour a worm that can cause a fatal human disease, are two typical examples. It is when fear becomes so obsessive that it begins to dominate our thoughts and cripple the running of our lives that it becomes an affliction. The fear of death stems from the physical body that quite properly strives for its survival, but there comes a time for it to be left behind. Without this law there would be an intolerable burden of population in the world. The older group would then either cling to power for as long as possible and block the way for the younger generation, or, more probably, be supplanted by the stronger, more vigorous young, and forced to spend endless years of increasingly futile retirement. This law applies to all life, but it is the peculiar gift of creative awareness that makes it especially poignant to the human. We are indeed made in the divine image (Gen. 1.26), and our work here is to actualize that image at least in some measure. When the outer vehicle, the physical body, has had its day, it has to be shed for a further advance of the true self, or soul. This, at any rate, is the general religious perspective, albeit expressed with different emphases by the various world faiths.

As we approach death, whether in youth or old age, so the consciousness of the soul gradually overshadows that of the body, which seems to slip away quite unobtrusively. But there are some people who cannot let go of the body in their thoughts: without it they feel depersonalized. It is the fear of total extinction that, I believe, oppresses those who have a morbid fear of death. I suspect that we all harbour that dread deep with the unconscious, no matter how strongly we may deny it. Clinging to mortal life is essential for our spiritual growth, and suicide is rightly frowned upon - though no one should judge, however leniently, a fellow-creature's actions until one can join them in the agony that may have occasioned the act of self-destruction. There needs to be a balance between survival of the body in the present moment and a wider view that sees mortal life as a preparation for further growth in an after-life state. The atheistic humanist, to be sure, could not entertain the possibility of any life of the person beyond death, but an atheist too, could balance the importance of survival now against inevitable self-extinction, as part of the wider process of life. This detached philosophical, indeed stoical, attitude is by no means to be deprecated, but I feel it does not do justice to deeper elements of spiritual intuition that are part of the normal human personality. An old soldier, a veteran of the First World War, once said to me that there were no atheists behind the trenches: when one's head was liable to be blown off at any time, one's mind, to quote Samuel Johnson again, was quite concentrated, and the divine presence was something more than a focus of wishful thinking.

We might then wonder why so many people, often morally sensitive and mentally astute, profess at least an agnosticism if not a frank atheism. I believe there are strongly emotional reasons for most people's intellectual rejection of God, even if they claim that modern scientific and psychological understanding has made this hypothesis unnecessary. It may be that they were disappointed in their expectations, that the God presented to them in their childhood did not make life as easy for them as they had been promised. Bad religious practice has also turned many people away from the Deity, for the character of some ministers and teachers of religion often fails to reflect the God whom they claim to serve; all the great world religions have their murky side of obscurantism, fanaticism, and persecution, to say nothing of collaborating at times with the ruling class to the detriment of the common people.

But there are two even more profound reasons why people reject God. First there is the intellectually intractable problem of a good, powerful God allowing the terrible tragedies in the world – how could he have remained silent during the terrible periods of genocide in our own century, to say nothing of the individual tragedies of little children being abused or dying of cancer? It would seem that, if he exists at all, he is either incompetent in his creation or else a heartless monster. The second reason for rejecting God follows on directly from this thought, and is relevant to our overall concern, the fear of death. The world religions all promise punishment in the after-life for those who

offend God, whose names are not written in the Book of
Life, to quote a Christian example derived from prior
Jewish teaching (Dan. 12.1 and Rev. 20.12). A number
of Jesus' parables portray a terrible fate for the unsaved
person in the after-life: the three parables that make up
Matthew chapter 25 spell it out very clearly. There is a
total rejection of the foolish bridesmaids ('virgins'); a
condemnation of the unprofitable servant in the parable
of the talents, who is thrown out into the dark, where
there will be wailing and gnashing of teeth (this
metaphor is also found in Matthew 8.12; 13.42 and 50;
22.13; and 24.51); while those who have lived uncharitable lives in the parable of the Last Judgement
(the Sheep and the Goats) will be cursed and sent to the
eternal fire that is ready for the devil and his angels.
But who of us is so sure of our virtue, for we have all
had our dark moments? Christianity, of all the religions,
preaches forgiveness. This is based on the atonement
made for us all by Christ suspended on the cross of
human evil, but there is still in many devout believers a
remaining guilt for past actions, even after they have
obtained absolution after confession either to God
directly or through the mediation of a priest. In the
past this was a powerful cause of the fear of death
among very devout people, but nowadays it is much
less common, especially as so many of the population of
the developed countries have lost direct contact with
their religious heritage, except in times of trouble when
God emerges once more from the obscurity of the past
to be 'our refuge and stronghold, a timely help in
trouble' (Ps. 46.1).

The problem with the concept of a severely punishing
God is that there seems to be no room allowed for our
own natural infirmities. Returning to the parable of the
Last Judgement, it is quite possible that an uncharitable
person had no charity shown to them during their
childhood, which may have been unspeakably vile.
While this thought does not justify their uncharitable

attitude to their fellow creatures, it ought at least to modify the judgement given at the end of the day. Any judge sentencing a criminal first finds out the circumstances of the person before pronouncing the sentence. One would hope at least as much from God, all of whose creatures have defects of one type or another, as part of their learning and growth into full personhood. The cruelly punitive God preached in some revivalistic rallies may shock rather unhappy, guilt-ridden people into 'declaring for Christ', but this God offends the sensitivity of more discerning listeners, who feel, possibly rightly, that they can do without such a being in their lives.

In the end we are wise to accept that we do fear the advent of death, at least on a purely biological level. Some people suffer from this fear for many years, as did Samuel Johnson; and it does not help them merely to rationalize it, because it is a deep emotional response that transcends the reason. The statement in 1 John 4.18 that perfect love banishes fear, suggests a way through the darkness: one should practise contemplative prayer, in the course of which one may, by the grace of God, know his presence by feeling his love. In the final analysis it is the ego that fears extinction, but when it knows the love of God in the silence of wordless prayer, it may be filled with that love and move beyond itself to the full nature of reality, a nature already 'encoded' (to use a biological term) in the soul. When such a person is facing death, it is most important for them to be supported by the constant presence of friends. I remember with sadness an aged nun who came to me for spiritual direction and confession. She had been at one time the mother of her community, and was overburdened with guilt which I believe was an emotional problem rather than the result of a past sin. I used to stress that she was forgiven each time I saw her, but although she expressed great gratitude for my kindness on each occasion, the obsession persisted. She was very fearful of death, which was close behind her. When she lay dying, so I was told, she was left alone for most of the time. Members of the community looked in fairly frequently, but no one stayed with the dear woman in her distress – such a small circumstance can indeed show how little love there is in even a religious community. But before I make a superior judgement, I cast my mind back to how desultory my visits were to a great friend of mine who was severely confused after a fall on her face in the residential home where she spent her last days. Of course I had many other matters to concern me, and conversation with her was unprofitable because of her combined deafness and mental confusion, but I see now how much more patient and gracious I could have been. She suffered for eighteen months before she died. If possible there should be a relay of attendants around the death-bed until the final coma, and then a more stringent vigil may be observed. However, just to emphasize the variety of responses to death, we have all probably known some people who prefer, in clear awareness, to die alone. It is not impossible that they are in conversation with a presence far beyond our vision on this side of the divide.

A last thought concerns how and when to tell someone that death is close at hand. Quite often this matter embarrasses medical attendants, close relatives and patient alike. On many occasions both relatives and patient know the situation, but in order to spare each other distress they subtly evade the issue. Some believe it is wrong to deny the patient the conscious experience of dying by withholding this information for as long as possible. On the other hand, many experienced medical practitioners have witnessed some patients collapse into a state of hopelessness when insensitively confronted with the imminence of their death. It is evident to me that there is no one correct answer to this dilemma; each patient must be treated as an individual. When we are quiet in humility, the Holy Spirit tends to make himself known to us and give us guidance. An instance I still remember concerns a dear friend, a man of deep spiritual awareness, whose life had been devoted to the rehabilitation of broken young men. In his eightieth year he fell victim to lung cancer and was slowly deteriorating in hospital. He seemed to have no insight into the gravity of his condition despite his severe breathlessness and weakness, and I felt it right to bring him gently to the reality of the situation. He suddenly said to me, 'I'm not going to die, am I?' I was shattered, and could only blurt out some insincere reassurance to him – and here was a person of deep spirituality, quite experienced in death and concepts of personal survival after it. He died quietly ten days later, and I have reason to believe that all went on well for him afterwards.

This slight episode from real life made me see how little we really know about the inner being of even those we love deeply. And how little one knows about the timing of any future event! God does move in a mysterious way, and if we are wise we fall in with the greater design by being constantly aware of the present situation and working diligently within it. Those engaged in the ministry of healing have an advantage over the purely scientifically-orientated practitioner. They work in terms of hope, not of mortality. But all the arms of healing ought to work together, because none is complete on its own. The sacraments of the Church and individual healing gifts serve to potentiate the effect of medical therapy. Occasionally they appear to effect a remarkable improvement in the course of a fatal disease, but more often they simply support the patient and relatives during a dark period. Sometimes death is accelerated, but is beautifully peaceful and brings with it an atmosphere of calm benediction that later plays its part in the spiritual training of those left behind to confront the experience of bereavement.

In the course of this chapter the word 'God' has

appeared quite frequently, but what do we actually
mean by it? In fact, the supreme reality is beyond
definition, just as Moses was merely given the vast yet
obscure title, 'I am that I am' (Exod. 3.14). If I
personally were asked by an interested, but totally
uncommitted, observer what I meant by the word God,
I would say 'a presence of spiritual aspiration beyond
myself by which my life is guided towards the light.'
Any more positive definition confuses the divine
mystery in a mass of human reasoning and verbiage.
The light towards which God guides me is embraced in
the three ultimate values: beauty, truth and goodness,
as declared by Plato. The Christian would prefer to
substitute the quality of love for goodness, but the
intention is the same; a mode of self-transcendence in
which we are part of the vast body of creation in a glory
that both obliterates the little ego and brings the full
person into unique actualization as a servant of love for
the whole community. Compared with this vision, all
earthly rewards are mere incidents on the way, neither
to be spurned nor to be desired. If they are desired they
soon become an end in themselves, subtly replacing the
divine vision with imprisonment in material substance.
But, fully realized, these same rewards are beacons on
the way to material resurrection whereby death is
swallowed up in victory (1 Cor. 15.54).

Note
A recent helpful addition to the vast mass of literature on the topic
of terminal care is *Mud and Stars, The Impact of Hospice
Experience on the Church's Ministry of Healing*, the Report of a
Working Party (Sobell Publications 1991). It is admirably simple
to follow, has a fully Christian basis, and provides many recent
references.

CHAPTER 6

The Near-Death Experience

Over the centuries there has been an accumulation of remarkable accounts of people who have had a narrow encounter with death, sometimes during the course of an acute illness (usually a heart attack), and sometimes after such trauma as a road-traffic accident, a fall while mountaineering, near-drowning, a battle injury, or a thwarted suicide attempt (if this should indeed be classed as an accident). To the observer these people appear to have died, and are currently described as 'clinically dead', but, far from giving up the ghost, their state of awareness is decidedly more acute than normally. Indeed, they seem to be receiving knowledge hidden from those attending to their bodily condition. The subject attained world-wide attention after Raymond Moody's book *Life After Life* was published in 1975.

The essence of a near-death experience is a completely changed state of consciousness in which the person is aware of the self in a mode of being far less limited to the physical body and its surroundings than is the normal situation. The awareness soars to other realms of existence and also deepens to confront a moral appraisal of past attitudes in the light of a clearer view of reality. The current authority on the subject, Kenneth Ring, a Professor of Psychology at the University of Connecticut, has deduced a five-stage account of the experience; while only some go through the whole process, most are more likely to know the earlier stages only.

First there is a feeling of deep peace and a sense of well-being far out of context with the state of the physical body. Then comes an awareness of separation

from the body, which bears the character of a typical
out-of-body experience (see later in this chapter). Many
people are able to 'look down on' their body and its
surroundings; their sight and hearing seem particularly
acute and their mental state is one of detachment. The
third stage is called by Ring 'transitional', since he
regards it as a transition between this world and what
may follow. It consists of a release with a sense of
travelling through a dark space likened to a tunnel. As
this stage progresses there is often an awareness that a
momentous choice has to be made: either a return to
the body or else an onward journey. While this
awareness of choice can occur elsewhere in the experience, it is especially typical of this stage of the process.
There may also be a life review in which all, or at least
part, of the previous life is seen in the form of vivid and
practically instantaneous images. The recall is generally
positive, there being no reproach or condemnation but
rather a sense of detachment. About a quarter of people
experience this life review, in the course of which a
'presence' is sensed or inferred but not directly seen.
This presence may speak, but more usually there is a
telepathic type of communication which relates to the
impending decision to return or to proceed. In addition
there may be an encounter with the souls ('spirits') of
deceased loved ones. The choice is made, often directed
by the tutelary presence, and there is a rapid return to
the damaged body.

Some people do not face the decision at the third
stage, but instead enter a fourth stage of seeing a light;
the darkness is replaced by a brilliant golden light
which may envelop the person or else draw him or her
into it. The light is usually not accompanied by any
presence. Many people interpret this stage as the end of
the dying experience and the beginning of a new life. In
the fifth stage the person enters into the light, which is
like entering a world of incomparable beauty. It is little

wonder that the traveller is loath to return to the earth after this experience, but there is a deeper knowledge that something has still to be accomplished here before the final transition can be made.

The question remains: is the near-death experience a presage of the life beyond death which we intuitively expect, or is it merely a system of impressive hallucinations produced by a badly damaged brain? In this respect an hallucination may be defined as an apparent perception of an external object that is not actually present. If the contents of the near-death experience were purely illusory, they might be determined by cultural conditioning or religious expectations. In fact, the light described in the experience has a numinous quality, and tends to be identified with God, Christ, the Buddha, or some other source of holiness, depending on the religious tradition of the person experiencing it. It is noteworthy in this respect that the scheme and content of the near-death experience is constant, irrespective of the beliefs, or lack of them, of the individual. But whereas the believer will find strength and confirmation in what has been experienced, the committed atheist tends to be shaken into questioning what may have previously been assumed, even to the point of exploring the metaphysical scene.

Hallucinations are characteristically varied, frequently bizarre, and above all idiosyncratic (peculiar to the particular individual). Their content is inconstant, and they usually occur in wakeful consciousness; by contrast, the near-death experience occurs in the clinically dead. Nevertheless, it is well recognized that some of the features of this experience can be attributed to the effect of hypoxia (a decreased oxygen content) on the brain, especially the limbic system of the temporal lobes. It is in this area that emotions are processed, just as in the occipital lobes the visual impressions from the retinas of the eyes are processed into meaningful

images. The feeling of deep peace, the experience of
being out of one's body, and even the experience of a
life review and communication with a presence, are all
compatible with an unusual response of the limbic
system to the hypoxia which follows the cessation of
the heart's activity. Similar sorts of sensations have
been reported in people with temporal-lobe epilepsy and
with tumours on that part of the brain. It could indeed
be strongly argued that the whole near-death experience
is a built-in response of the psyche to the unexpected
threat of imminent bodily destruction. The fear of
suddenly realizing one is about to die without due
warning would be mercifully palliated by this neuro-
psychological reflex. There is, however, one aspect of
the experience that cannot be so easily explained as
pure illusion, and this concerns the out-of-body experience.

The out-of-body experience is essentially one of
feeling that one's consciousness is temporarily outside
one's body. It is estimated that about one-quarter of
the population have had such an experience, sometimes
in association with injury (as in the near-death scene),
when the out-of-body experience is described as induced
or enforced. On other occasions the experience is quite
spontaneous, as when the person is relaxing in bed or
sitting down to study; in this case the experience is
called natural. Some subjects have a special tendency
towards out-of-body experiences, and a few can provoke
them at will. These provide excellent material for parapsychological investigation.

The actual experience could easily be dismissed as a
special type of hallucination. The British psychologist
Susan Blackmore has suggested that the out-of-body
experience stems from a disruption of the mental image
one has of one's body and how it is placed in the
immediate environment. Normally we take this position-
ing for granted, for with it we can do our work safely in

the present situation. The body image is under constant adjustment according to the information of a continuous sensory input. If, however, there is a sudden disruption of the sensory input, as for instance after an accident, the mind may have difficulty in maintaining the body image. It may be that the brain tries to put together an approximation of what the body image should be when sensory information is disrupted, and an out-of-body hallucination results. Such an explanation accords more happily with the enforced experience than with the natural one, in which there is little evidence of a serious sensory shutdown.

The theory, furthermore, does not explain the not infrequent acquisition of information that could not have come through the senses, from the memory, or even by inference, that is part of some out-of-body experiences. For instance, an anaesthetized patient on the operating table may witness things elsewhere in the surgical theatre that would be quite beyond the range of vision of a person in that situation, and may also report snippets of conversation among the theatre attendants. Occasions have been known when this capacity to view at a distance has extended even further afield from the person's present point of vantage. This is particularly the case in some near-death experiences. This greatly enhanced consciousness is the most cogent indication that the near-death experience has an intrinsic validity that out-distances any possible element of pure hallucination. The person who has had such an experience out of the body is convinced that the soul can travel free from that body. It needs to be said that any such experience is relayed back to the body through the limbic system of the brain's temporal lobes; while we are alive in the flesh, even if 'clinically dead', we function as a psychosomatic unit. The point at issue is whether the experience originates in the brain or is merely transmitted through the brain from some outside source. In the case of sight, we know that the eye receives the visual impressions and the occipital lobes of the brain process them, as has already been mentioned. When it comes to extrasensory impressions, like those typical of the near-death experience, we cannot be so certain, since these are private and therefore not capable of confirmation by other people. But the enhanced consciousness typical of the near-death experience must challenge the limited view of materialistic reality. 'We are greater than we know', as Wordsworth puts it in the 'Valedictory Sonnet to the River Duddon'.

Kenneth Ring has also investigated the near-death experience from a more sociological and psychological point of view. He found that about a third of those who come close to death report the experience, whereas the remainder appear ignorant of it. He found that the type of person who is able to dissociate from a present circumstance is more open to other realities. Such a person may have undergone severe emotional suffering in childhood – an example would be the victim of child abuse. A person who has learned to respond to a menacing situation by spontaneously dissociating from it, is more likely to enter into a different state of consciousness which not only shields them from the immediate threat but also discloses an alternate reality. However, some individuals seem to have an innate capacity for dissociation, irrespective of their background. It could be that the near-death experience may be more frequent than is supposed, but only a minority of people remember it. The situation would then be comparable with dreaming: modern dream research using rapid eye movement sleep patterns has shown that everybody dreams in the course of a night's sleep, but we know from personal experience that not everyone remembers their dreams.

An interesting point for consideration is the moral

nature of the near-death experience. It may disturb believers that a committed atheist seems to be as eligible for the heavenly vision as they themselves. Here we must remember that even among the devotees of religion, there is at times a severe failing in love, whereas an atheist may be more acutely attuned to the suffering of the community. Jesus amplifies this theme in Matthew 7.21-3, reminding us that merely affirming God is not enough, and that even charismatic gifts used in his name do not automatically gain his recognition. What matters is the state of the person's heart, for one can still be evil while using the correct approach. The story of Simon Magus amplifies this truth (Acts 8.9-24).

However, at least one investigator has pointed to a less pleasant aspect of the near-death experience. Maurice Rawlings, an American clinical psychologist who worked in a cardiac resuscitation unit, reported a number of patients who had had terrifying experiences, and screamed for help as evil, dark beings came to drag them away. This observation so impressed Rawlings that he became a Christian believer.

This may also shed some light on those cases of clinically dead people who on resuscitation have no memory of any experience. A terrifying experience could be dealt with by the mind shutting down on it as if to deny its occurrence. This is common in abused children; a surface depression may be all that is left to mark the event, and psychotherapy is necessary to reach the actual cause of the problem. It is nevertheless surprising that Rawlings' observations have not been recorded by other workers. The blissful aspect of the near-death experience is certainly the one that is fully recognized.

Whatever the view of agnostics, there is no doubt that the near-death experience radically changes the mental perspective of a person. Life takes on a new meaning, the concept of growth into a reality that

transcends material satisfaction is now accepted not
merely as a religious teaching but as an urgent fact of
life. There is no longer any fear of death, but at the
same time life on earth is valued much more preciously
than before. This is because a purpose to one's life is
now divined, dimly but definitely. In the same way the
person who has survived a suicide attempt realizes that
this was the wrong thing to do, and is unlikely to
succumb to the temptation a second time. A belief in an
after-life is much stronger; at the same time the person
is filled with a greater tolerance, compassion and loving
concern than was ever experienced before. A decidedly
more universal view of religion is also common, so that,
without renouncing a prior denominational allegiance,
the person is more open to spiritual insights from other
sources. In fact, the insights obtained during the
experience help to expand tolerance and inform the
understanding to new levels of service and growth of
the personality.

Some of those who return to earth after a near-death
experience are quite angry, and a few refuse to accept
their return for some time. They insist that they are
dead – psychiatrists call it the 'I-am-dead syndrome'. It
may take weeks or even months to decondition such a
person. All this proves how glorious most near-death
experiences are, and how they convince their recipients
of a greater promise to life than merely our comparatively
brief earthly spell. In fact, the near-death experience
cannot be taken to prove survival of death, because the
clinically dead person is still alive in the body, including
the limbic system of the temporal lobes of the brain
which register the emotionally comforting part of the
experience. The question remains as to whether these
experiences originate in the brain or are merely registered
there from some outside source. The expanded consciousness typical of the out-of-body experience does indeed
seem to go beyond the domains of the brain, and

remains the most cogent argument that the person was at least in contact with other sources of intelligence than purely material ones.

Notes

The early publication that sparked off interest in near-death experiences was:

R. A. Moody, *Life after Life* (Harrisburg, PA, Stackpole Books 1976).

More contemporary accounts are:

R. Broughton, *Parapsychology – the Controversial Science* (New York, Ballantine Books 1991). Chapter 8 includes a good account of near-death and out-of-body experiences.

K. Ring, 'Paranormal Antecedents and Aftereffects of Near-death Experiences: Findings from New Research', *American Society for Psychical Research (ASPR) Newsletter* XVII, 3 (1991).

S. Blackmore, 'Near-Death Experiences: In or Out of the Body?', *Skeptical Inquirer*, vol. 16, 34 (1991).

CHAPTER 7

Dying:
The Liberation of the Soul

As a person moves beyond the field of mortal conflict
with disease or injury to the final phase of separation
from the body, so does the mental state change. Both
the fear and the sense of rebellion that may have been
felt earlier, that occasioned a fight to the death for
survival, now wane. The individual becomes quieter,
more tranquil, and clearly at rest. Admittedly, some of
the peacefulness of the terminally ill is due to the drugs
administered to alleviate pain and emotional distress,
but in addition there is a blessed peace resulting from
frank exhaustion, the consequence of the prolonged
battle for survival which is being slowly but inexorably
lost: the time for withdrawal elicits an attitude of quiet
acceptance. The soul has probably become progressively
detached from its accompanying physical body during
the terminal phase of life on earth, and it is the body
that alone is registering the signs of failing function
which were mentioned in chapter 5. As has already
been remarked, the effect of that dysfunction is
probably very much more distressing to those in
attendance than to the person who is making the great
transition.

Our attitude to the dying person should be one of
silent respect. It is insensitive, if not frankly dis-
courteous, to be subjecting the dying person to our own
religious views, or conjuring up our own special vision
of the after-life. Indeed, the experienced friend becomes
increasingly humble and silent while sitting with the
dying person. To be sure, at an earlier stage of the
process of renunciation of the body the individual may

ponder on philosophical or theological questions about the fundamental cause of the fatal condition and the possibility of an after-life state. In this case it is right to impart our own insights and beliefs as humbly and tentatively as possible; it can never be wrong to affirm strongly one's personal convictions about personal survival, but in the end it is one's demeanour and inner sanctity that is most likely to support the dying person on the way forward. Those who are very vociferous are often, albeit unconsciously, hiding from their own uncertainty under a barrage of scriptural quotations. As Jesus told Nicodemus in their strange nocturnal meeting, 'In very truth I tell you, we speak of what we know, and testify to what we have seen, and yet you all reject our testimony' (John 3.11). The type of person who categorically disdains the testimony of anyone professing a belief in personal survival, who dogmatically asserts that there is no purpose to anybody's life outside the brief period of sojourn in this world, is one who is not in contact with his or her real self, or soul, that can whisper of a knowledge of intimate relationships far beyond the limits of human reason. In the lovely words of *The Cloud of Unknowing*, 'By love may he be gotten and holden, but by thought never.' To return to the passage in St John's Gospel, one would feel that Nicodemus, unlike his peers, did have direct knowledge of his soul. The testimony of John 7.50-2, and especially John 19.38-42, where his labour with Joseph of Arimathaea in burying the body of Jesus in the garden tomb is noted, is very moving. Those who reject the testimony shown by Christ in life and death are often arrogant, being sure of their own intellectual accomplishments. In the statement of Christ recorded above it would seem that he was addressing us all in the person of the perplexed, honest seeker after truth, Nicodemus.

When someone committed to the spiritual life,

especially a follower of Christ, is destined to die young
from a relentlessly progressive disease, or as the result
of an accident innocently sustained, he or she (or the
kind relatives or friends) may suspect that the suffering
results from some serious, if overlooked, sin, and is the
consequent punishment meted out by the unrelenting
God of justice. Such a presentation of God is found
throughout the scriptures, especially in the Old
Testament and in some of Jesus' more unremitting
statements and parables like the three in Matthew 25,
already mentioned. To many sensitive people it is
beyond belief that a God of mercy and love, such as is
revealed in the life of Christ, could allow any of his
creatures to be treated in this way. Nevertheless it is
good that such a person should discuss all that is
troubling them with a sympathetic friend, and especially
a minister of religion if there is a denominational loyalty.
The sacrament of absolution, or reconciliation as it is
especially happily called in the Catholic Church, can
have a great healing power, whether for further service
in this world or as a preparation for what is to come in
the life beyond death. It is common for people of
aspiring spirituality to be especially aware of their
failings, and this is quite right: the closer we approach
the divine mystery, the more sharply focused is our
past life with its previously overlooked peccadilloes
that can easily be magnified into major sins. Another
way of stating the case is to see the holy person as
taking on the mantle of the tax-gatherer as described so
starkly in the parable of Luke 18.9-14. This thought
finds a parallel in Jesus' crucifixion between the two
criminals with whom the hostile crowd joyfully identified
him. Great saints have been known to say on their
death-beds, 'O Lord, I am unworthy.' And God has
replied to them, 'Yes, but I am worthy,' worthy even to
take their sins upon himself as did Jesus in his ministry.

There is a mystery about apparently unmerited
suffering and death at an early age that can only be

fathomed, at least to some degree, by going through the experience personally. St Paul sheds a ray of light on this agonizing matter in Colossians 1.24, where he writes, 'It is now my joy to suffer for you; for the sake of Christ's body, the church, I am completing what still remains for Christ to suffer in my own person.' Two observations need to be made here. First, Paul does not claim to add to the redemptive work wrought by Christ, which cannot be increased, but he gives of himself as a martyred missionary of the faith, so that in the end all the world may know the Saviour's name and bow down to it in a transformed way of life. Secondly, there is the ever-present danger of masochism, a perverted sexual stimulation by inflicting pain on oneself, if a person's intensity of action becomes too dominant in their life. We need a sense of humour, so that our dedicated activity does not finally serve to nourish the devil and his works; unremitting anger that boils over into hatred of people with other views and lifestyles is a warning signal.

Considering all this in terms of the innocent suffering around us, it could well be that we are all in such close psychic fellowship with each other and with the creation universally that we cannot avoid taking on the sufferings of others, especially if we are psychically open and spiritually aspiring. Vulnerability is the price we pay for spiritual understanding; only thus can we serve our fellows with that love that Jesus showed during his ministry. It is indeed a terrifying thing to fall into the hands of the living God (Heb. 10.31). A person of deep spirituality takes their suffering as a matter of daily life; thus the individual can share in the pain of the world and lift it up to God for relief and eventual healing. Likewise there is little fear of approaching death – if anything, in fact, a sense of pleasant relief tinged with joyful expectation.

In fact, as the dying person slowly relinquishes the body, it is as if the previous struggle to keep going on is replaced by a merciful drift on an escalator provided by an unseen source. The person is carried passively along; nothing is required of them except quiet obedience, which is fully forthcoming as the physical vehicle is being left behind. The concept of a soul that can outlive the physical body amuses the materialist, who jibs at the thought of a ghost in the machine that escapes when the body dies. But a far more satisfactory model is that of an overlying intelligence which makes itself known through the body, and then detaches itself when the body dies. A comparison with a musical instrumentalist is helpful; when the instrument is damaged even the finest virtuoso can produce no sound. It is good if the dying person is close to God in awareness. In a hospice situation this milieu is available to everyone making the great journey, even if the name of the Deity remains unmentioned. Loving care is much closer to the divine source than even fulsome religious language. But if the dying person is a believer, so much the better for then the name of God is close at hand; the Catholic practice of giving the person the Last Rites of the Church is an excellent way of preparing the dying person for the journey and confrontation ahead.

In fact, of course, we should be aware of God at all times, for no one knows when the great transition is to begin. It is in this respect that the fundamentally decent person has the final advantage over their heedless, selfish fellow: the former is close to God in everyday life, whereas the latter is far from any thought except that of immediate sensual satisfaction. When the body, with its senses, is left behind, what does such an individual possess in the life ahead? Or, to quote Mark 8.36 once again, 'What does anyone gain by winning the whole world at the cost of his life?' What we are at heart shows itself to us as we leave the flesh behind and are opened involuntarily to a new consciousness of reality. It is certainly best to be close to God in thought at all times, but even if this ideal state has not been attained (it is a product of an assiduous prayer life), it is good to remember the divine name as one passes from this life to the next. We will consider the implications of this later on.

As the dying person slowly relinquishes the body, so other perceptions may impinge on the consciousness, encouraging the person on the mysterious journey ahead by the assurance that there is company on the way. It has been known for a long time that dying people sometimes have hallucinations of their friends and relatives who are already dead. Not unnaturally these cases are inevitably dismissed out of hand by sceptics and agnostic observers as the products of a diseased brain, damaged by drugs and the internal waste-products that accumulate as the body's metabolism fails. Others would attribute them to wish-fulfilling fantasies in people who cannot face the obviously logical fact of personal annihilation when the body dies. The situation here bears a strong resemblance to the near-death experience and its explanation in terms of brain dysfunction or a psychological defence mechanism, mentioned in chapter 6. But as with the near-death experience, there is one finding that is anomalous and cannot be adequately explained on a purely physical basis. Cases have been reported in which the dying person actually 'saw' someone 'on the other side' whom he or she believed to be alive in the flesh, and who had in fact died only very recently and whose demise was unknown to all those present with the dying one. We have previously defined an hallucination as an apparent perception of an external object that is not actually present (chapter 6), but this essentially private sensory experience could on occasion be valid for the person concerned. The field of parapsychology contains numerous examples of 'phantasms of the living', and similar appearances involving the dead are also well known. Inasmuch as these phenomena are sporadic and cannot be produced at will, they tend to be written off by scientifically trained people, but in the end it is personal experience that counts in the lives of us all. To quote the hackneyed observation from *Hamlet*, 'There are more things in heaven and earth, Horatio, than are dreamt of in your philosophy.' This statement arouses derision in the person of the world, but as death draws near, the mind tends to broaden as new data are fed unceremoniously into it.

In fact, the pendulum is beginning to swing in favour of those who take these phenomena seriously. One of the chief investigators in this field is Karlis Osis, who was Director of Research of the American Society for Psychical Research. His interest dated from 1961 when he published his first pilot study of death-bed hallucinations, and later he extended his original research and substantiated his findings. He sent a detailed questionnaire to a large number of doctors and nurses about the death-bed visions described by their patients. Of course only patients who were conscious during their last hours of earthly life were suitable for this investigation. In the patients studied, apparitions from the life beyond death were common. They could not be attributed to medical factors, since those who had obvious brain damage, drug overdosage, or toxaemia did not register this type of hallucination. The types of hallucinations seen amongst such patients were rambling, confused, and above all related to the world (such as reliving past memories, for example a quarrel with a close relative). Those who had other-worldly visions were clear in mind, notwithstanding their proximity to death. Nor could the visions be attributed to wish-fulfilment. They were spontaneous, and occurred as often in patients who expected to recover as in those who thought they were going to die. A wish-fulfilling vision might have been expected to conjure up the image of a living relative who was too far away to visit the dying patient; in only a very small proportion of cases was a desired living person hallucinated.

One of the most interesting features of the figure who appeared from 'the other side' was that it often came with the definite purpose of taking away the dying person. Osis calls this a 'take-away' figure, and he found that in those cases where death occurred within ten minutes of seeing the apparition, the 'take-away' figure was strongly predominant. Usually the 'take-away' figure was someone the patient knew, and he or she was glad to receive its beckoning call, but sometimes there was a shrinking away in terror, the dying one being violently opposed to going away with the 'visitor'. Nevertheless, the patient was invariably taken away. Osis found that there was no relationship between these hallucinations and the patient's inner conflicts or the emotional preoccupations on the day preceding the hallucination; thus Freud's 'day-residue principle' (imagery reflecting memories of previous experience) could not be satisfactorily invoked as an explanation for this interesting phenomenon. Studies were conducted in the United States with its predominantly Judaeo-Christian world-view, and in India where Hinduism and Islam predominated. The apparitions of death, especially the 'take-away' figure, occurred similarly in both cultures, though neither the Bible nor the Bhagavadgita mentions this aspect of dying. Osis also found that these death-bed visions tended to evoke an inner illumination in the patient. While the relatives wept, the dying one was 'lit up'. Some showed a serenity suggesting 'the peace which passes all understanding' with which the priest often blesses the congregation at the end of the Eucharist. One might expect to find such a state of benediction in association with an other-worldly awareness. Many parapsychologists believe that this type of experience is one of the most suggestive pointers to the probability of survival of death, especially when it is taken in conjunction with the near-death experience.

It is interesting that a 'take-away' figure of a rather

different complexion is met with in Teutonic folklore: this is the bearded, golden-crowned 'erl-king' who lures little children to the land of death. He is the subject of one of Schubert's most famous songs: a father rides his dying child home on horseback, and while he speeds ahead the child is terrified by the vision of the erl-king. The father tries to soothe his child, but the vision persists, the awesome erl-king calling the little one with frightening power to depart with him. When the father does return home, he finds his child dead. This is, of course, merely a legendary encounter, but legends too have their origin in some sort of real experience. One remembers from Pascal's *Pensées*, *'Console-toi, tu ne me chercherais pas si tu ne m'avais trouvé'* (Comfort yourself, you would not seek me if you had not found me). This is both a 'proof' of God's existence (an aspect of the so-called 'ontological argument') and an indication that there are aspects of psychical reality that are deeply hidden in the soul, but liable to reveal themselves in times of emergency.

Having said all this there remains yet another caveat: what is the validity, to say nothing of the authority, of the 'take-away' figure, or for that matter the contents of the near-death experience? Fundamentalist Christians of all the three great communions, Orthodox, Catholic and Reformed, would unite in attributing demonic presences at work in order to delude the patient that all is well, whereas in fact they have no reason to be sanguine. We will come across this objection throughout the whole psychic field, fertilized as it is by the stern prohibitions against necromancy that are found in the Pentateuch. In the end we have to come to our own judgement, not neglecting either scripture or the tradition of the Church, but also bearing in mind that neither of these two sources is without its incompleteness, which has shown itself in terrible massacres and persecutions that are the reproach of Christianity (and of religious tradition in general). Speaking personally, I believe that the great criterion is love, a word so great in implication that people like us are only on the foothills of its understanding. And yet it is shown daily by an unlearned mother who will give up her very life in caring for her children. With this example in view, I cannot but feel that the typical contents of both the near-death experience and the 'take-away' figure, in the dying person, are at the very least a source of support for what is to come. The changed person that emerges from the near-death experience and the serenity of the dying one taken further on by the private visitor cannot in my view be anything but a blessing.

At this point I feel it is right to impart some of my private experiences with the dying at the point of their great transition. I have always had a peculiarly strong affinity with those who are soon to die, of whom cancer victims form the majority. I have discovered that my work does not end with my last visit, for on more than one occasion I have been aware, during my sleep, of accompanying them to the threshold of the after-life, popularly symbolized as a door. They have been admitted but I have been repeatedly turned back. I have always envied these departing souls, for I have known that existence 'on the other side' is much easier than it is here. In this respect we recall the near-death experience when the 'clinically dead' person is sent back to this world to complete unfinished business. I am especially glad to learn that my work in this field is not unique, for at least one other person told me quite spontaneously of her similar experiences, and she is a person of considerable intellectual stature who is an authority on the near-death experience.

It is evident that certain people with a special type of spirituality help the onward passage of those whom they had known well in this life. A fairly non-attached person like me would be more helpful than a grieving relative or friend. I seem to supplement the action of the 'take-away' figure (whom I have never met in the course of this work). I have been aware of my function on quite a number of occasions, more than one of which occurred when I did not expect the imminent demise of the sick person. Indeed, my experience was then confirmed by subsequent news about the individual's death. It could well be that this accompanying function is accomplished best during deep, undisturbed sleep when one would, of course, be completely unaware of what one was doing on a deeper psychic level. As in all spiritual work, the ego has to be silenced before God can do his work on and through the soul.

It seems right to conclude this section by recalling St Paul's account of a mystical experience he himself had had:

> I know a Christian man who fourteen years ago (whether in the body or out of the body, I do not know - God knows) was caught up as far as the third heaven. And I know that this same man (whether in the body or apart from the body, I do not know - God knows) was caught up into paradise, and heard words so secret that human lips may not repeat them. (2 Cor. 12.2-4)

This is an interesting comment on the conflict between the Greek view of the soul's immortality and the Hebraic understanding of the soul and body being one composite whole. It could well be that this is true of the incarnated person, but at the time of bodily disintegration the soul's independence is demonstrated as it moves to new fields of experience. If survival of death is the truth, one would expect this to be the case, unless one holds to the primitive view that the body itself rises on 'the last day' after having lain in the earth for perhaps many centuries, if not millennia. Considering that nothing of the body eventually remains except the bare skeleton – the fleshy parts providing nurture for the creatures of the soil – it would be a miracle of miracles for the whole person to be assembled as he or she was in this life, and presumably now in a healthy young body. Bodily resurrection, to which I fully assent, has a different meaning for me; it is the raising up of the physical body to spiritual essence, as shown in the changes wrought in Jesus from the time of his burial through the period of resurrection up to his final mystical ascension to the heavenly realm. For the remainder of humankind this resurrection is contingent on the full resurrection of the universe, which 'is to be freed from the shackles of mortality and is to enter upon the glorious liberty of the children of God' (Rom. 8.21). Another way of expressing this apocalyptic vision, one which we shall later consider, is: 'Flesh and blood can never possess the kingdom of God, the perishable cannot possess the imperishable' (1 Cor. 15.50).

Notes

Two important accounts of death-bed visions are:

K. Osis, *Deathbed Observations by Physicians and Nurses*, Parapsychological Monographs no. 3 (New York, Parapsychology Foundation 1961).

K. Osis, 'What Did the Dying See?', *ASPR Newsletter*, 1975.

A recent very useful book on an even wider field of 'nearing death awareness' is:

Maggie Callanan and Patricia Kelley, *Final Gifts, Understanding and Helping the Dying* (New York, Poseidon Press, and London, Hodder & Stoughton 1992).

SURVIVAL

—⟶ ⟵—

*So it is with the resurrection of the dead: what is
sown as a perishable thing is raised imperishable.
Sown in humiliation, it is raised in glory; sown
in weakness, it is raised in power; sown a physical
body, it is raised a spiritual body.*

1 Corinthians 15.42–4

CHAPTER 8

Survival of Death:
A Consideration

From what I have already written it is clear not only that I accept a life beyond mortal death but that I also believe I am actively involved in helping some dying people beyond the barrier, even if I personally am not permitted to cross over with them. But is personal survival of such great importance in the first place?

The concern for a life beyond death arrives very late in the Old Testament. Its absence from the writings of Isaiah, Jeremiah and Ezekiel in no way lessens the authority of their moral teaching, even if they hold that all individuals, good and bad alike, are destined for the shadowy underworld of Sheol (or Hades in the Greek tradition). This appears to be a realm of insubstantial beings in an atmosphere of dull torpor – suffering does not seem to be present, possibly because personality as such is no more. In the account of King Saul's visit to the woman of En-dor, obviously a fine medium, it transpires that a prophet even as auspicious as Samuel is to be located there (1 Sam. 28.8–20). In fact, deep thought about the after-life has never been a major concern of the Jews. Their involvement with the here and now has made them the dynamic people that they are, and has in no way diminished their witness to the things of the mind and the spirit. A minuscule group, a product of their own tendency to form a separate community and of the consequent vicious persecution by their neighbours, they are at the hub of the worlds of scientific research and artistic performance. Belief in personal survival is built into the theology and liturgy of Judaism, but it is not a prominent part of the everyday concerns of the people themselves.

From this consideration it is evident that powerful spiritual teaching and living are compatible with a considerable disinterest about personal survival of death. And this is right; it would be improper for people to live a good life on earth only with an eye to substantial heavenly rewards. In fact, such a life would not be good, for its egoism would compare favourably with that of the Pharisee in the parable of Luke 18.9-14. As the great philosophers have taught us, virtue is its own reward, a doctrine hard to accept for us ordinary mortals, like the labourers in the vineyard in Jesus' parable (Matt. 20.1-16). Those who labour for many hours get the same salary as those who come in late; inasmuch as the early workers had agreed on their payment in advance, they are simply getting their due, but in comparison with those who come late it does seem rather hard that somehow their longer toil is not duly recognized. Had they been more spiritually aware, they would have been grateful for the advantage of a day's steady employment, something the later workers had to forgo as they stood around idle and faceless until their presence, too, was acknowledged. It is a privilege to be able to have a definite employment: to work well in whatever capacity laid down for us by the fortunes of life is to serve God and our fellow creatures. As we forget ourselves in the performance of the work, so we enter into a knowledge of eternity. A rather different approach to this same reflection is contained in the famous prayer of the Sufi saint Rabi'a, 'O God! if I worship Thee in fear of Hell, burn me in Hell; and if I worship Thee in hope of Paradise, exclude me from Paradise, but if I worship Thee for Thine own sake, withhold not Thine Everlasting Beauty!' One begins to know this beauty by acting in love in the present moment; as the ego consciousness is transcended, so we give God a chance to enter our lives.

These considerations are important when we recall

the hostile, but very pertinent, criticisms of religion by
Marx and Freud. Both in their own way saw religion as
a means of evading the demands and suffering of this
world by its tendency to promise another, and kinder,
life somewhere when we have quitted this one. To Freud
such a life was pure illusion, while Marx compared
religion to opium that relieves the pain of humanity in a
heartless world. As any medical practitioner would
know, the relief of pain does not cure the fundamental
complaint, and indeed if irresponsibly sought can serve
to obscure the cause of the trouble, so as to delay
dealing with the condition properly. Freud saw the
treatment in terms of psychological maturation, whereas
Marx prescribed the economic reorganization of society
according to his own radical socialistic principles
contained in the *Communist Manifesto*. Excellent in
theory, its practice proved a failure in the various
countries of eastern Europe. There is clearly a gap
between intellectual theorizing, no matter how well-
intentioned, and human nature; the latter cannot simply
be tailored to fit in with the demands of the former. St
Paul remarked on this dichotomy in Romans 7.21-3.
He also saw the only possible way out of the tragic
impasse: openness to God's action on the personality,
whereby we are moved from mere carnal self-concern to
the foothills of spiritual transformation.

This is the point of spiritual development and the
purpose of the religious quest: to become a finer person
in a better society. Jesus put it thus: 'I have come that
they may have life, and may have it in all its fullness'
(John 10.10). This is a life that sees beyond the
exigencies of the world without in any way evading
mundane issues. It reaches to eternity, seen as the
perfect action done in the present moment. As we have
already quoted Hebrews 10.31, 'It is a terrifying thing
to fall into the hands of the living God.' But this terror
is also the way into an existence that far transcends

any earthly limitation; it brings the earth into a heavenly context. Far from escaping the world, the spiritual consciousness infuses each moment with a significance that endures long after the event has passed into the pages of an unwritten history. The Marxist and Freudian condemnations apply to bad religion, one that coerces the person into conformity by threats of punishment for any disobedience, especially the fear of exclusion from a state of heavenly bliss. The authority of a religious tradition then subtly excludes the living God from the lives of its believers. But a person who knows the living God now has indeed passed from death to life, because a love flows out to all creatures (and not only fellow-Christians as is stated in this otherwise perfect criterion of 1 John 3.14, though to be practical we start with what we already know and move towards the unknown as our life unfolds).

It is in this context that personal survival of death is very important. Even if our lives on earth have been as exemplary as that of Job before his fall, we, like him after that event, are still mere children in the school of life. He was privileged, as a reward for his steadfast honesty and courage in the face of his terrible adversity, to see God as creator as closely as befits the human understanding. We, unlike this fictional character, need to grow into that understanding much more slowly, so that we can accommodate supreme spiritual knowledge as our capacity increases. Even Jesus himself needed about thirty years of spiritual training before he was ready for his great ministry. If the saints are especially aware of their unworthiness as they die, how much more is this the case with us lesser mortals! If our life is indeed snuffed out at the end of even a long mortal tenure, all that we have achieved in personal growth and spiritual wisdom disappears with us. Our training and work have no tangible end except the education of those who follow us, and their end is in turn equally unproductive of personal growth in a larger context. Survival of bodily death is part of the development of the personality in the greater context of eternity, a state of being that transcends time and space, and is with us now as fully as it will be when we die. The hope is that in that post-mortem state we will be nearer in our own consciousness to eternity than we are while limited by a material world, but this depends on our own spiritual growth while on earth.

A final thought concerns the admissibility of the human to question the deep things of God, as allegedly revealed in the world's holy scriptures. Inasmuch as the human was created in the image of God (Gen. 1.26-8) and given dominion over the other animals, and indeed all the world's creation, for good and for evil depending on the moral responsibility of the individual, it follows that the human mind is permitted to penetrate the most intimate details of God's creative acts in the universe. The marvels of scientific research multiplying day by day emphasize this intellectual mastery. Furthermore, the human has been given the supreme capacity for knowing God as closely as is commensurate with the consciousness of the soul. The world's great mystics are able to tell us as much as is within the range of human communication about the love and power of the Creator. The human has a god-like capacity, by which I mean a focus of will that can direct the individual's life into a personally selected path. In Psalm 82, an invective against corrupt judges, even they are called gods, sons of the Most High; but their end will be a mortal one (verses 6-7).

St Thomas Aquinas said, '*Impossible est naturale desiderium esse inane*' (It is impossible that a natural craving should be a delusion). When the human at the height of love cannot bear the thought of any of God's creatures being eternally damned or absolutely annihilated, such a person is attaining something of the love of

Christ, whose ministry on earth was devoted to revealing the Kingdom of God by works of healing and deliverance. It is not in fact impossible that our purest longings could be a conspiracy to deceive us, but it is intolerable. In the end we have to behave like responsible adults, making our own decisions. Where love is clearly contravened we have a perfect right to object, while at the same time admitting that we are mere clods of ignorance before the inscrutable wisdom of the Most High. All we can trust is that our noblest thoughts and kindest feelings are directed by Christ, who is the way, the truth and the life (John 14.6).

CHAPTER 9

Survival of Death: Intimations

It is right that we should look to the survival of some part of the personality after bodily death; it is the soul, or true self, that goes on, for, as St Paul says, 'Flesh and blood can never possess the kingdom of heaven' (1 Cor. 15.50). Should we, however, seek directly for proof? The warnings against getting in touch with the dead, and indeed against using any form of divination, are clear-cut in the Pentateuch: 'Do not resort to ghosts and spirits or make yourselves unclean by seeking them out' (Lev. 19.31), and 'Let no one be found among you . . . who casts spells or traffics with ghosts and spirits, and no necromancer' (Deut. 18.10, 11). Similar interdictions are found in Leviticus 19.26; 20.6, 27. We can see only too clearly the reason behind these injunctions: once one enters the psychic world one lays oneself open to an indiscriminate group of influences, most of which are probably benign and even helpful, but a few of which are demonic in origin and destructive of the personality in effect. Just as we would not dream of discussing our most intimate affairs with a fellow traveller on public transport, so we should be even more careful about trafficking with unseen 'spirits' on the other side of life, which incidentally is part of our environment in the present world also. This is why divination is fraught with danger. Yet the use of lots was sanctioned in the affair concerning King Saul and his son Jonathan (1 Sam. 14.41-2); these, however, were sacred lots the care of which was reserved for the levitical priests, and the practice was discontinued after the reign of David. Lots were also used in deciding the apostle who was to replace Judas Iscariot (Acts 1.26).

From these examples it seems clear to me that the use of psychic gifts and exploration into the unseen world is acceptable if done in the name of God, which implies the call and guidance of the Deity. It is when the ego consciousness takes charge, demanding results for the individual irrespective of any higher concern, that a hazard lies in wait. But alas, our motives are tragically mixed (to recall Romans 7.21-3 yet again), and therefore psychic investigation is best left to those who are well grounded in Christ and have a basic sensitivity. All this is relevant to another danger inherent in the psychic field: a temptation to lose sight of the Deity amid the welter of intermediate entities that may present themselves. Some may be accorded an almost god-like status by enthusiasts, but few are frankly malicious. The whole practice tends so often to trivialize the world beyond death. There is, of course, also the danger of demonic infestation, one lying in wait especially for solitary explorers of low intelligence working with the ouija-board and similar pieces of equipment that seem to attract entities of low character. It seems clear that the psychic field should be left to qualified parapsychologists who understand the unconscious realm of the mind; if they have a spiritual base, so much the better.

But if it is wise not to explore this psychic area of reality, it is not uncommon for its inhabitants to come spontaneously to us, both from living sources and from the regions beyond mortal death. In this case the burden of psychic sensitivity is borne heavily on our consciousness, and we cannot simply evade its implications.

The three pieces of evidence that point most clearly to survival of death are: first, direct communications from the other side of death; secondly, the work of mediums; and thirdly, memories of past lives suggestive of reincarnation. Proof may continually evade us because psychic phenomena are notoriously sporadic; like the Holy Spirit, which is their ultimate mediator, they are like the wind blowing where it wills: we hear its sound but cannot determine either its source or its destination (John 3.8). Scientific research into psychic phenomena is very difficult, since reproducibility, the very essence of what science as we understand it demands, is rare to obtain. Furthermore, the emotional attitude of the research worker is important; if there is a basic hostility to belief in the psychic realm, the capacity of the tested subject (whether a medium or one who claims special gifts of telepathy or clairvoyance) is severely repressed. This is perhaps less damaging to parapsychology now than previously, inasmuch as the discipline of nuclear physics, dealing with ultimate particles of matter and their dispersal in space, also recognizes the part played by the observer in the experiment. On a more mundane level, we may consider the concert pianist playing to an appreciative audience in a hall. Then suppose the performer and instrument were transported into a place of entertainment such as a public house. If the performer were rash enough to play there, the audience would soon make its displeasure felt, at the very least by loud conversation. It is improbable that the performance would attain any result other than general exasperation and ultimate chaos. This imaginary situation makes obvious the personal element in studies of human behaviour. In the above example, while the performer enriches the audience, they in turn support the performer. The studied objectivity of the scientific method is not adequate to deal with such a situation, which is then quite correctly placed outside the orbit of traditional science.

Nevertheless, psychic phenomena have an intrinsic validity known to far too many people to be summarily dismissed as illusion. Two quotations are relevant here.

The first is from the celebrated nineteenth-century scientist Thomas Henry Huxley in a letter to Charles Kingsley: 'Sit down before fact like a little child, be prepared to give up every preconceived notion, follow humbly to wherever and to whatever abysses nature leads you, or you will learn nothing.' Only a small company of scientists, not alas including Huxley, have been prepared to acknowledge the existence of the psychic realm and experiment with its progeny. This is because its existence would challenge many dogmas of materialism which classical science accepts as a necessary foundation. Human emotion soon blocks an unconditional search for truth.

The second quotation, from the eighteenth-century philosopher Immanuel Kant, is more encouraging: 'The same ignorance makes me unwilling to deny utterly the truth in divers ghost stories, because I have a curious reservation that, although I doubt each one by itself, when they are considered as a group I have some belief in them.' This quotation, taken from Professor Ian Stevenson's book *Children Who Remember Previous Lives* (which we shall consider further on), takes for granted that the material is meticulously collected and reported and that the workers are people of the utmost probity, for parapsychological research has repeatedly borne the stigma of a dishonest bias in reporting cases favourable to the worker's particular point of view. The same applies to the work of those involved in scientific disciplines, but here the results can be challenged by experiments or observations made in other laboratories (including the greatest of all places of research, the world in which we live).

As regards the first piece of evidence pointing to a life beyond death, direct communication from the other side of life, a distinguished parapsychologist of the last century, Frederic Myers, recognized three main classes of 'messages': sensory hallucinations, emotional impulses and impulses to action, and finally, definite intellectual information. Extrasensory perception (also called ESP and *psi*) between the living also falls into one of these three categories. The classic collection of these cases is contained in *Phantasms of the Living* by Edmund Gurney, F. W. H. Myers and Frank Podmore; published in 1886, it was the first authoritative study of *psi* made by the Society for Psychical Research. Though more than a century old and not without its flaws, this collection remains the basis of all subsequent studies of direct communications between humans. Gurney had noted that nearly three-quarters of the apparent *psi* experiences in *Phantasms of the Living* either coincided with the agent's death or very shortly followed it. This might be seen as indirect evidence of survival, suggesting, as it seems to, the presence of an inner principle within the human frame which is capable of being freed from the restriction of the physical body to make contact with distant friends at the time of that body's death. Such cases could alternatively be explained as telepathy between the dying person's mind and that of the percipient, usually remaining latent for some time in the unconscious before its impact reveals itself. But sometimes the apparition is seen months, or even years, after the agent's death. In the best attested cases there is a clear purpose in this communication, perhaps a signal of unwaning love frustrated to the point of suicide, or else an attempt to show the percipient some money, a will, or other valuable commodity hidden in the dead person's belongings.

Love and death seem to be the precipitating factors in most direct communication purporting to come from the after-life, but an agnostic can easily invoke the uncharted powers of *psi* to explain the communications, such as telepathy (the direct communication between two minds), clairvoyance (extrasensory perception, usually of an object, without the mediation of another person's mind), precognition (a knowledge of the future that is direct and not inferred from present information) and retrocognition (a similar knowledge of the past). Telepathy and clairvoyance are means of acquiring knowledge of contemporary events, whereas precognition and retrocognition deal respectively with the future and the past. It must be admitted that many people deny the existence of such psychical processes: coincidence can be invoked to explain apparent telepathic communication between two people, while a past emotional association could bring the mind to a sudden jolt when a future possibility or a past situation is suddenly confronted; a hidden memory can easily be brought to consciousness by an unexpected emotional stimulus, which might then coincide with a dramatic glimpse into the past or the future. Few of those who have experienced these modes of *psi* would be seriously disturbed by these arguments, largely because of the frequency of the phenomena in sensitive people and also the not-infrequent importance of what is revealed. A little experience is worth more than endless learned debate; but, of course, the experience must be properly evaluated by competent parapsychologists. Some experiences are symptoms of mental abnormality, while much more frequently the recipients embellish what they have received with details provided by the imagination. There is a difference between perception and apperception, which is the action or fact of a perception already experienced becoming conscious by one's reflecting upon it. In this way a perception is united and assimilated into a body of ideas already possessed, and so comprehended and interpreted. Sometimes, as we have already noted in chapter 7, it is the dying person who may see a friend, perhaps in the function of a 'take-away' figure, of whose demise he or she and those in attendance knew nothing.

The second piece of evidence pointing to an after-life

comes from the work of mediums, or sensitives as they are often called because of the prejudice against mediumship found in the Bible. Mediumship is quite different from witchcraft, though many natural mediums have in past times been burnt at the stake, accused by the Church of being witches and trafficking in black magic. The ignorance has been as profound as the reaction has been brutal. A medium is one who claims to obtain communications that appear to have originated in the minds of deceased people who are conceived of as still living in a discarnate (physically bodiless) state. While it may be wrong according to scripture to initiate communication with our loved ones, it sometimes happens that an individual has an innate mediumistic faculty, which, I believe, it would be wrong merely to ignore. Like the servants in the parable of the Talents, we are expected to use our gifts and not simply hide them in the ground (Matt. 25.14-30).

A medium is able to undergo a dissociation of consciousness during which another personality, called the control or guide, takes charge and produces information about matters both in this world and in other realms that are completely hidden from the person (and the rest of us) in normal consciousness. The medium may enter a state of trance or else remain in normal consciousness. In the course of a 'sitting' a deceased member may reveal such solicitude, as well as more personal facts, and sometimes traits as well, that the sitter believes in the full existence of the entity as a surviving link with the person so well-known before physical death.

Mediums are of all types and grades, from the barely literate to a few highly educated people who would not care for the label 'medium' and prefer to keep their faculty a secret from all except specialist parapsychologists. As Rosalind Heywood writes in her excellent book *The Sixth Sense*, the great medium is rarer than the great artist, and we are fortunate if half a dozen crop up in a century. There have been only three available for lengthy study by the Society for Psychical Research since its foundation in 1882: Mrs Eleanore Piper, Mrs Willett (the pseudonym of an aristocratic lady) and Mrs Gladys Osborne Leonard, all of whom deserve perpetual recognition for the help they gave to parapsychologists. And yet their undoubtedly veridical communications could all be attributed to *psi* with living sources, not only people who knew the deceased ones (especially Myers, Gurney and Hodgson, one of the original team) but also to documents and other sources of information. This is called the 'super-psi-hypothesis' of mediumistic knowledge of the dead as opposed to the 'survival hypothesis'. In our present state of knowledge it is not possible to make a categorical judgement; much depends on one's own intuition, coloured as it so often is by rationalistic or religious prejudice or by spiritualistic sympathies.

Personally I believe that these three mediums were indeed frequently in communication with discarnate sources, but from time to time the channel became disturbed, and confusing information was transmitted (the means of communication are either verbal or else by automatic handwriting). With a lower class of medium this confusion tends to become more prominent as intruding entities interfere with genuine communication. These entities are usually benign, but sometimes a more unpleasant source reveals itself. Furthermore, the medium will tend to acquire telepathic information from the sitter's unconscious, a complication especially found in the deep mourning period of bereavement. Added to this is the temptation to fraud, an allegation especially favoured by rationalists and some devout religious believers. Fraud is by definition a conscious act aimed at deceiving its victim, in this case into believing that there is a genuine communication with a deceased member, when in fact details have already been known by the medium or have been subtly extracted from the sitter before or during the sitting. When all these factors are borne in mind, it is clear that investigating mediumship is best left to those who know the field well. The finest mediums acknowledge that they are supporting a desperately lonely person in the throes of grief, and work towards an emancipation from the past loss to a future competence. It is what they are that tells, much more than what they believe from 'the other side'.

In my view mediums have a distinctive part to play in the scheme of things: by communication with those in a state of hell (which we shall consider later), in order to help them to move to the intermediate, or purgatorial, state. This they do by their very presence; if they are people of devout prayer, they can play a very important part in the life of the world to come. I regard with less enthusiasm their attempts to bring fellowship between the deceased and their loved ones still on earth, though, of course, direct proof of personal survival would have a revolutionary effect on human behaviour. But at the same time the cutting edge of faith, by which we grow spiritually, would be severely blunted. It could well be that we are not yet spiritually developed enough to know the way of death and of becoming what we are meant to be.

Meanwhile the process of 'channelling' goes on apace; this is simply mediumship in which a source of self-proclaimed authority gives an impressive series of lectures to a dedicated group of sitters who are taught many things about the after-life and exhorted to live as virtuously as possible now in their present situation. While one can seldom fault the material that is published, one can hardly ignore its 'intermediary' character; it does not lift one up as do the great mystical works, or inspire one like the world's scriptures.

Nevertheless, many people obtain sustenance from channelled material that seems to be denied them in places of worship. It is probable that such writing contains the germ of greater truths. It accepts survival of the personality as a matter of fact, but does not offer any proof.

It is notable that the three great mediums mentioned earlier on lived at the end of the last century and in the first fifty years of this one. There has been no significant work on mediumship and its relationship to personal survival for well over fifty years. As the time moves on, so more and more doubt is cast on the original findings, a situation almost inevitable in parapsychological research where so much depends on personal testimony. The reputations of the dead are very easily smeared by later biographers. The dead cannot reply, but we can hope that their concerns are far greater than the nastiness of our little world. It is open to doubt whether any modern mediums would add to the riches of data provided by their illustrious predecessors.

Notes
Reliable books on parapsychology are:
R. Heywood, *The Sixth Sense: An Inquiry into Extra-Sensory Perception* (London, Pan Books 1971). Also published as *Beyond the Reach of Sense* (New York, E. P. Dutton 1974).
I. Gratton-Guiness, ed., *Psychical Research: A Guide to its History, Principles and Practices* (Wellingborough, Aquarian Press 1982).
B. B. Wolman, ed., *Handbook of Parapsychology* (New York, Van Nostrand Reinhold 1977; reprinted Jefferson, NC, McFarland 1986).
A good study on channelling is:
A. Hastings, *With the Tongues of Men and Angels: A Study of Channeling* (Fort Worth, Holt Rinehart and Winston 1991).

CHAPTER 10

Survival of Death: ?Multiple Lives

The third piece of evidence pointing to survival of the personality after mortal death is the claim by some people to remember past lives on earth. This implies that the human personality, or a component of it, may survive death, and later, perhaps after an interval spent in some non-physical realm, become associated with another physical body. This definition, taken from Ian Stevenson's book *Children Who Remember Previous Lives*, is the essence of reincarnation, a belief intrinsic to the Hindu, Sikh and Buddhist religions, and also widely held among many inhabitants of West Africa and East Africa (who have not been converted to Christianity or Islam), north-western North America, some Shiite Muslims of Western Asia (despite Islamic rejection of the belief) and the Druse people of the Lebanon. It is the Semitic religions, Judaism, Christianity and Islam, at least in their orthodox tradition, that have categorically denied the possibility of reincarnation. It is nevertheless of interest that from 20 to 25 per cent of unchurched (and sometimes churched as well) people in western Europe believe in the concept of reincarnation. In the great majority of cases, it is doubtful that they learned of it from external sources; at the most these served to ignite an already latent belief.

If indeed there is truth in the concept of reincarnation, the crux of proof lies in acquiring genuine memories of past lives from those now living in the flesh. Quite a number of adults claim such a memory, but the possibility of this having been stimulated and augmented by the present memory, through books and

other encounters, is too strong for anyone else to take
these statements at more than face value. The same
must largely be said about alleged reincarnational
memories uncovered by hypnotic regression techniques,
a practice at present very fashionable in some circles.
The full meaning and explanation of hypnosis is still
unclear, but it seems that in this state the person's
attention becomes concentrated and the mind freed
from extraneous and intruding thoughts. And so it
becomes possible to focus on a particular aspect of the
past with vivid clarity. But in the process the hypnotist
achieves the power to direct the subject's thoughts; if
there is a direct injunction to remember something
which cannot in fact be done accurately, the subject is
liable to produce an incorrect answer in order to please
the hypnotist; thus truth and falsehood are easily
intermixed.

The process can occur also when the subject is
commanded to return to a previous life. In this peculiar
state of compliance the subject may provide any sort of
account, embellished by historical facts and literary
fiction based on historical details. There is also a
heightened power of dramatization, so that the various
latent items of information in the mind are linked and
animated into a 'previous personality'. As Ian Stevenson
points out, the process has much in common with
dreaming; it is the glamour attached to hypnosis,
especially in its stage presentations, that has led to the
belief in its infallible capacity to recover memories. The
historical anachronisms associated with many 'previous
personalities' cannot but make the observer smile.
Sometimes, when asked, the subject will refer to a
special book that produced a deep impression. Information once acquired can be completely forgotten until it
is uncovered by hypnosis or dreaming; this is called
cryptomnesia. It is possible that truly reincarnational
material is evoked during hypnosis, but the admixture

of other material makes it hard to evaluate. One of the best researched examples of hypnotic regression uncovering a plausibly reincarnational past is recounted in Morey Bernstein's *The Search for Bridey Murphy*, in which the subject gave many correct details of life in early nineteenth-century Ireland. Unfortunately the person herself remained unidentified, so that a reincarnational basis cannot be proved. Occasionally subjects under hypnotic regression speak a language foreign to them; this is called xenoglossy.

A further pointer to a past life, at least in the mind of the individual, is the feeling of having been at a new locality on a previous occasion. This is called a *déjà vu* experience, but is usually best explained in terms of a precognitive dream which is subsequently forgotten though residues of it lie just below the threshold of consciousness. On other occasions the present scene may be very similar to one already experienced, so that one feels one has been there before. Some especially vivid dreams may have a reincarnational component; they tend to recur, and have a logical sequence absent in the usual dream, but once again there is no positive proof that they stem from a past life. It is also evident that adults are unsuitable subjects for reincarnational studies. What is needed is a virgin mind such as small children possess, uncontaminated as yet by worldly concerns.

Dr Ian Stevenson, Carlson Professor of Psychiatry and Director of the Division of Personality Studies (formerly the Division of Parapsychology) at the University of Virginia at Charlottesville, is the foremost investigator of reincarnation cases. In 1961 he started investigating a famous case in the Indian state of Uttar Pradesh. Here a three-year-old boy peremptorily identified himself with a Brahmin family and described a member of it as his father. He showed a remarkable knowledge of the locality where the family lived, and also more intimate facts about the habits of the family. The real father of his extraordinary son, a lawyer by profession, saw to it that all the facts were witnessed by seven friends and colleagues at the high court. The previous father, whose name the boy knew well, was approached by means of a letter in the principal English-language newspaper for the area. He was found to be living in Benares City, and when the real father took his son to Benares, the boy found his own way with ease to the home where he once claimed to have lived. A son of the Brahmin family had indeed died several years previously. A most significant fact in this account (and in many others besides) is that the child acted the part that he claimed, in this case of a Brahmin, right at the beginning, ordering his motor car to be ready for use, as if the considerably poorer father just had vehicles at his disposal (the affair occurred in 1926).

Of course, Stevenson could only review the records of this case, which occurred thirty-five years before his own investigations began, but as a result of a contemporary investigation he was able in 1966 to write his first book on the subject, *Twenty Cases Suggestive of Reincarnation.* The main facts were very similar to the above: statements about the previous life by the child and associated unusual behaviour. A birthmark or birth defect, corresponding either to what the previous person bore or how he or she later died, was not uncommon. To me the most compelling evidence is the anomalous behaviour of the child; even if the past life was learned (a most unlikely situation), it is remarkable that the child should persist in the corresponding habit pattern. A return to the present norm would be much more convenient for all the parties concerned. It has been suggested that parents of a lower caste in India might feel socially exalted to have an 'ex-Brahmin' living with them, especially when the child could introduce them to his former parents in the course of their investigations. The reverse is more true: the demands made upon them by their exacting child could be a distinct nuisance, so much so that the recollection of a past life is not welcomed by many Hindu families. The child's attachment to the past memory usually persists for from three to six years, after which he or she gradually ceases to care about the past and becomes more attuned to the present life. An interesting complication occurs when there is a change in sex from the past life: the child may hold on to its previous sexuality quite doggedly for a long time - a girl, for instance, pursuing the physical activities of a boy for quite a number of years - but eventually the proper sexual status is attained.

An obvious criticism of Stevenson's early publications is that the case material came exclusively from social groups that accepted reincarnation; it could reasonably be argued that the parents of children who remembered a past life would at least be sympathetic even if they did not encourage the phenomenon. By contrast, Christians, Muslims and Jews, to say nothing of the vast numbers of 'scientific' unbelievers in the developed countries of the world, would actively discourage any reincarnational accounts among their offspring, or at least scoff at them until the children had learned better manners. But Stevenson has not been idle in his researches, and has now found examples of children with reincarnational memories who are resident in western Europe (including England) and the United States. In these cases the parents previously did not believe that reincarnation was possible, or else were part of a religious culture violently opposed to the idea. But it must be conceded that the bulk of Stevenson's material comes from social groups that do accept the concept; he himself believes it is more common than is acknowledged in Europe, the United States and Canada, but is often disregarded by the parents of the children

who claim memories, simply because they do not
understand the significance of what they are receiving.
Indeed, part of Stevenson's work is to bring this fact to
the notice of parents, so that, if they do pick up
anything unusual, they can report it to his team at
once, before the childhood memory is blurred by
contingent material from the present time.

Stevenson's method is to interview the subject and
all firsthand witnesses where possible. Gradually he
interviews important informants several times, partly
to elicit additional information, but also to test the
consistency of their reports over a period of time. He
also checks hospital records, birth certificates and any
other sources, to substantiate details of the witnesses'
accounts. Eventually he accumulates enough evidence
for a thorough account of relevant facts of the case as
well as a good estimate of the credibility of the
witnesses. The next step is to see if the child's memories
correspond to the life of a particular individual who had
died before the child's birth. Often this will have been
done by relatives or friends by the time Stevenson
hears about the case, so he will repeat the interviews
and investigations with relatives of the alleged previous
personality. In some cases Stevenson, or his colleagues,
has been instrumental in making the identification. At
present he has mobilized over two thousand cases of
children who remember previous lives. He wisely
describes all these as cases that 'suggest' recincarnation,
but he defends them vigorously against dismissive
normal explanations.

The first possible explanation of these cases is that
they simply arise from childhood fantasies; children
often develop imaginary playmates at about the same
age as reincarnational memories show themselves. But
such memories are specific and detailed, and can be
later verified, unlike the vague, fragmentary childhood
fantasy, which cannot be verified. A fantasy would not

lead a child to the location of a former personality or to identify former relatives. Admittedly, a reincarnational fantasy could be encouraged in a sympathetic environment, but an increasing number of cases are being found in neutral or hostile families, as we have already seen.

Another possibility is that the child has acquired the information normally from its parents or other adults, or else from the common stream of human communication. The two families may have met before the case was investigated, and the child's vague statements of the previous life may thus have become unintentionally strengthened. Behavioural traits of the previous personality may have been cued by the adults and learned by the child. But in fact, in many cases, the detailed information that was communicated by the child was simply not available in the house where the child lived. In enough cases a substantial distance separated the families, and written records of the child's statements were made before they ever met – if indeed they ever did meet. It should not be forgotten that many cases of alleged reincarnational memories arise almost as soon as the child is able to talk.

The final explanation brings in *psi* – a 'super-*psi*-hypothesis' of grand proportions: the child somehow picked up information about the previous personality from surviving relatives and friends. But why should there be a cluster of *psi* cognitions about a particular individual, one among thousands who have died in recent years, while the subject shows no evidence of any other *psi* experiences? Quite often the previous personality had been dead for some considerable period, and mourning was over. Often the child's source of information is apparently more than one person, since the various facts are known only by different individuals.

There is a final observation to queer the pitch: in a small number of cases the subject was born before the

person whose life he or she remembered died. In
Stevenson's series the interval varied from a day or two
to several years. This would seem to indicate a sort of
possession. It would be easier to explain away such
awkward cases as caused by an error in recording dates,
but in some instances this was clearly not the case. The
usual interval between the previous personality's death
and the subject's birth is rather less than three years –
a median interval for 616 cases from ten different
cultures was fifteen months.

It is evident that Ian Stevenson has made the concept
of reincarnation much more believable, for his cases
certainly point in that direction. However, many more
cases from Europe and European communities in the
United States, Canada and other parts of the world
need still to be discovered and investigated, for most
cases still come from the 'reincarnational hinterland'. It
will be good also if other parapsychological studies
from workers unrelated to the Stevenson team can be
made, and if the child subjects can be formally assessed
psychologically.

To many Christian believers such explorations into
suspect areas like mediumship and reincarnation as we
have made in the last two chapters, are at the very least
unnecessary to a person of real faith, if not possibly
damaging to faith. But if our faith is real, we ought to
be able to contain new domains of knowledge. Furthermore, the truth should be able to sustain our faith, for
no one knows when their present assurance may be
shattered by a future calamity. Doubt is an important
ingredient of a growing faith, a faith that is not afraid
to face the facts of life by participating in that life and
not moving off into a corner to enjoy a pleasant, if
illusory, sleep. In the memorable passage of 2 Peter
1.5-7, 'You should make every effort to add virtue to
your faith, knowledge to virtue, self-control to knowledge, fortitude to self-control, piety to fortitude,
brotherly affection to piety, and love to brotherly

affection.' We need never fear that knowledge, provided that our affections are God-centred. The disciple Thomas, who would not accept the resurrected Christ until he was given absolute proof of his identity (John 20.24-9), is our exemplar. To be sure, Thomas represents a particular type of person, one who uses his or her mind acutely and will not be side-tracked by automatic adoration; but that person should not be censured on this account.

To me the most important product of parapsychological studies is the fresh light they shed on the potentialities of human personality. We are indeed greater than we know, to quote Wordsworth again. Indeed, we hardly know ourselves at all in this life, so immersed are we in the passing scene, trying to gain the world but sacrificing our true integrity in the process. If the reincarnational hypothesis is true, at least for some mortals (as I suspect it is), it means that the soul, properly cleansed in the after-life, proceeds on its way in a completely fresh genetic system, there to learn ever more about life so as to distinguish the meretricious and transient from the wholesome and eternal.

A last respect must be paid to the objections of the religious fundamentalists, whom we mentioned in chapter 7 with reference to 'take-away' figures: are these data true in themselves or merely part of a great conspiracy organized by the demonic forces to deceive us into believing that a caring life exists beyond the grave even for the most arrant knave, who should according to various scriptural texts go straight to eternal damnation? Fortunately there are more encouraging texts in the Gospels that stress divine forgiveness: Luke 15 is a necessary corrective to Matthew 25, and it seems to me that both have to be taken in creative tension in the spirit in which they were recorded. Anything that brings us closer to love and forgiveness cannot be of demonic origin.

Notes

The important book on reincarnation is:

I. Stevenson, *Children Who Remember Previous Lives: a Question of Reincarnation* (Charlottesville, University Press of Virginia 1987).

An earlier one was:

I. Stevenson, *Twenty Cases Suggestive of Reincarnation* (New York, American Society for Psychical Research 1966).

Other useful contributions are:

R. Broughton, *Parapsychology - the Controversial Science* (New York, Ballantine Books 1991). Chapter 8 includes a useful resumé of Stevenson's work.

J. Matlock, 'Past Life Memory Case Studies', in Stanley Krippner, ed., *Advances in Parapsychological Research* 6 (Jefferson NC, McFarland 1990), pp. 184-267.

M. Bernstein, *The Search for Bridey Murphy* (New York, Lancer Books 1965; first published by Doubleday 1956). This reference has been included because the case has been alluded to in the text.

CHAPTER 11

Survival of Death:
Some Spiritual Perspectives

It is generally held by the world's great religious traditions that the life beyond death contains within it the seeds of judgement on how we have lived this life. Looked at in this perspective, it is no wonder that God kept the secrets of survival of death closely hidden from his chosen people. They were chosen, not to enjoy any special privileges, but to spread the knowledge of God to the whole world. This is, of course, the greatest of all privileges, but only when the scales of worldly blindness are lifted from one's eyes can one appreciate the full blessing of communion with the Most High. It is in this context that we can begin to appreciate the enormous difference between the various stages of survival that we have been considering and the life eternal that is the abode of spiritual reality. And so we can begin to understand the absence of teaching about the after-life in the Old Testament until less than two centuries before Christ. To be sure, the psalmists from time to time yearn for an unending fellowship with God, one that transcends the death of the body (Psalms 16.9-10, 49.15 and 73.23-4 articulate this hope, in contrast with 6.5, which states the traditional view very starkly).

It was the period of persecution under Antiochus Epiphanes which evoked the heroism of the Maccabean family and its numerous martyrs, that brought into being a more concrete view of the immediate survival of the personality. This is stated categorically in the Book of Daniel (12.2) written between 167 and 164 years before Christ, and in the Second Book of Maccabees (the thought inspires the whole of chapter 7), written some sixty years later. There arose a triumphant conviction of the life of the world to come, when the righteous will go to eternal glory and the unjust be condemned to eternal shame. The literal resurrection of the body is predicted, because Jewish thought at that stage could not envisage life without its powerful directing organ. However, the Book of Wisdom (the final book of the Old Testament and written towards the middle of the first century before Christ) teaches the Hellenic conception of the soul's immortality divested of its physical body. There has in fact been a continued tension in later Jewish thought between the concept of the resurrection of the whole person and the immortality of the soul, and Christianity has inherited this tension. I have given my views on the resurrection of the physical body in chapter 7, but the problem remains for many devout Jewish and Christian believers.

It is noteworthy that even at the time of Christ one major party of the Jews, the Sadducees, denied a resurrection because it was not taught in the Law of Moses (Mark 12.18-27). After Jesus' resurrection the life beyond death became a burning issue (the two essential words in the Christian faith are incarnation and resurrection), but St Paul's most detailed teaching on the subject, in 1 Corinthians 15, deals only with the period shortly after death. This seems to be because an imminent crisis was sensed: a vivid expectation of the end of the historic order, followed by a raising of the dead and the creation of an entirely new human world. When this apocalyptic vision failed to material-ize, a more material view of the person's destiny was envisaged. Perhaps the most fundamental Christian insight (and with it to a greater or lesser extent the Jewish and Islamic insights also) is what is called the 'linear' view of history, that history has an origin and an end, both rooted in the plan and power of God. It is here that there is a radical conflict with the reincarnational philosophies of Hinduism and Buddhism, which see existence as a cyclical phenomenon, in which the end of all thinking people is to escape the round of rebirth and enter the unitive state of Nirvina. The body has its eternal significance in Christian thinking, though what its 'resurrection' may mean is still a mystery. The resurrection of Jesus' body is clearly non-material, but the remainder of humanity do not show this amazing transformation, at least in our world.

In Christian belief, as shown in the New Testament, there is a judgement of universal scope at the end of history, pronounced by God; it is Christ, God's Word made flesh, who will embody and execute that judgement by coming to be visibly present in the world again at the end of history. Later on, it was also suggested that there was a judgement pronounced by God at the end of each individual's life. From Tertullian on, most Greek and Latin Patristic authors confidently accepted Platonic philosophical arguments that the soul, as the conscious and self-determining core of the human person, is indestructible, and so anticipates its eternal fate, through a preliminary personal judgement, from the moment of death. With this judgement comes retribution, a final state of human existence, one of permanent and perfect happiness for the good and permanent, all-consuming misery for the wicked. It was later seen that the heart of both beatitude and damnation is to be found in the relation of the human creature to God: in union we know perfect love; away from him there is self-destructive agony.

Furthermore, the blessed dead are still involved in the life of the Church, both in praying for the living and in experiencing the benefit of their prayers. This implies that there is a communion of saints, St Augustine asserting that the souls of the pious dead are not

separated from the Church, which even now is the
kingdom of Christ. Origen, one of the most adventurous
of the early Fathers, hoped for the salvation of all
spiritual creatures, as also did St Gregory of Nyssa and
Evagrius, but many others contested this. Augustine
had such a poor view of human nature that he assumed
that most people would not be saved and that even the
perseverance of believers in the life of grace was far
from assured. It is fascinating how both positions
continue to be proposed in our own time. Both remain
shrouded in the double mutually-limiting mystery of
God's providential love and the genuineness of human
freedom: the apposition of Luke 15 and Matthew 25,
with Luke 16.19-31 (the parable of Dives and Lazarus)
to remind us of the hard side of the Third Evangelist
also.

A deeper question remains: is the end of this life also
the end of change and self-determination, or is it
possible, after the body dies, for souls to grow in the
knowledge of and desire for God? Origen and Gregory
of Nyssa affirmed the latter, Gregory going so far as to
see beatitude consisting in continual progress towards
deeper union with God, corresponding with a continual
expansion of the human's capacity to know and desire
the Good. Related to this matter is the possibility of
purgation from sin after death. Such suffering was seen
by the Greeks and Jews as a way to wisdom (Prov.
3.11-12) and a personal means of expiating sin (Ps.
38.17-18). Origen likened suffering to a medicinal
process aimed at restoring all souls to their original
union with God, and suggested a long period of
purgation after death for those who, through the
inadequacy of their experience, had not been sufficiently
schooled during life. It seems clear that the foundation
for the belief in purgatory as a separate, interim state
for some souls, is first found in the earlier Greek and
Latin Patristic tradition. The concept of purgatory was
developed in Western medieval theology, but its roots

are seen much earlier. However, many of the Patristic authors opposed such a notion as denying the finality of death and the judgement of God. All this has been inherited by the Catholic and Protestant Churches even of our own time.

This vast scheme (which I have taken with gratitude from the Epilogue of Brian E. Daley's Handbook of Patristic Eschatology entitled *The Hope of the Early Church*) reminds us how little any of us know about God's scheme of universal redemption. But the early Christian believers were strengthened by their knowledge of the Risen Christ.

> Therefore, now that we have been justified through faith, we are at peace with God through our Lord Jesus Christ, who has given us access to that grace in which we now live; and we exult in the hope of the divine glory that is to be ours. More than this: we even exult in our present sufferings, because we know that suffering is a source of endurance, endurance of approval, and approval of hope. Such hope is no fantasy; through the Holy Spirit he has given us, God's love has flooded our hearts. (Rom. 5.1-5)

When we are with Christ we are in eternal light, but the process, disarmingly simple in terms of an individual encounter, needs to be embraced moment by moment. It is in this terrain that our consideration of aspects of the life beyond death is important.

Although the three Semitic religions are emphatically non-reincarnational in their orthodox formulations, there are a few passages in the Bible that dimly suggest some sort of pre-existence of the soul. An early one is Jeremiah 1.5: 'Before I formed you in the womb I chose you, and before you were born I consecrated you; I appointed you a prophet to the nations.' Psalm 139.16 has something of the same flavour: 'Your eyes foresaw my deeds, and they were all recorded in your book; my life was fashioned before it had come into being.' Rather

more explicit is Wisdom 8.20: 'I myself was noble, and
I entered into an unblemished body,' with a possible
reincarnational undertone (the text has also been
interpreted as simply affirming the superiority of the
soul over the body).

In the Gospels there are two passages that have
possible reincarnational undertones, neither of which is
very strong: Mark 9.11-13 (with its parallel Matthew
17.10-13) in which John the Baptist is identified with
Elijah, who has to return to restore all things before
the Messiah appears; and John 9.2-3, in connection
with the healing of a man born blind, and whose defect
is queried as being a result of something he or his
parents had done wrong. In the first passage it was the
function, not the person, of Elijah that John had fulfilled
(according to Malachi 4.5-6, the last sentences of the
canonical Old Testament); in the second passage Jesus
denies either possibility, at least in that particular case.
A more helpful passage is John 14.2: 'There are many
dwelling-places in my Father's house; if it were not so I
should have told you; for I am going to prepare a place
for you.' There is little in the Bible to refute reincarnation; the text, 'Just as it is our human lot to die once,
with judgement to follow, so Christ was offered once to
bear the sins of mankind' (Heb. 9.27-8), could be cited
against belief in reincarnation. But I personally accept
this on its face value as affirming the death we all have
to experience in this world with the subsequent
judgement (however we may conceive this) in the
after-life.

Of all the Church Fathers, Origen comes closest to
affirming reincarnation, but in fact he taught and wrote
about the pre-existence of the soul and its circumstances
at birth (whether incarnated into a healthy or unhealthy
body) being the reward or punishment for virtue or sin
in the soul's previous existence, an approach similar to
the karma of Hinduism and Buddhism. But this soul
existence was in the heavens and not the earth, nor did

it constitute one of a series of former lives. He does not speak about successive incarnations of the soul in various earthly bodies. Origen's advanced views about human destiny won for him a series of powerful enemies, and in AD 553 the Second Council of Constantinople adopted fifteen anathemas against poor Origen, dead for about three hundred years, and condemned the idea of the pre-existence of the soul. It is of note that, although a threatening person can be eradicated easily enough, the ideas of that individual are less easily dismissed. They can lie in abeyance for many centuries, but finally they will emerge and cause more of a stir than they would have had they been sensibly propagated by a well-schooled advocate. The Church's authority has been severely eroded by the foolish Galileo affair in the seventeenth century and by the more penetrating effects of the revolution in thought that has followed the researches of Charles Darwin into evolution and the origin of species in the nineteenth century. Only a determined fundamentalist can now take the Bible literally in many of its statements.

The obvious problem of the traditional Christian (and also Jewish and Islamic) scheme of the final things is the fate of the individual. It is shocking to contemplate the individual, a creature of God's love, being judged categorically for eternity according to the showing he or she has made in one lifetime. This is especially true for those who hold that only a privileged few attain heavenly status and the remainder are eternally damned. The saved are those who have accepted Christ (or Allah in the Islamic tradition) in terms of a theological formulation. In the conservative form of the Evangelical tradition the die is cast at the end of this short life as to whether a person is to go to heaven or to hell. Traditionally the hell is one of eternal retribution, but a more recent view is that the individual is annihilated either at death or at the moment of final judgement or after a period in hell. This alternative is called conditional immortality. Whatever view such an advocate takes, there is no need to pray for the dead: the saved do not need prayer, and the condemned are out of reach of any prayer. The broader Catholic tradition has wisely interposed a state of purgatory, the place of purification, between the hell and heaven of traditional Christian eschatology. It is in my opinion where most of us will find ourselves when we die, as I shall outline later.

When we consider the fate in store for the average individual at the time of conception, let alone birth, hemmed in by genetic determination and the emotional state of the mother, later to be extended to the full environment in which the child is reared, up to the time when that person is let free in the far from easy world, it becomes hard to attach categorical blame to any life. Those who enjoy a loving parental relationship in the midst of a happy family life are immeasurably privileged over the many more who have known no family stability in their childhood. But even here there is a caveat: does the family's love prepare the person for giving love to the undiscriminating world, or is it a seditious form of blackmail that would restrict the person's life to the *mores* and sympathies of a small social or racial group? It could be argued that the second form of attachment is not really love but only self-protective solicitude, but where does one draw the line? Jesus himself had to learn to curb his family's solicitude in the interests of a greater family around him (Mark 3.21, 31-5).

Those whose early lives have been blessed with wealth and a good education have opportunities denied to others whose upbringing has been desultory and their education unsatisfactory. We in the West can hardly envisage the abject poverty in India and much of Africa and Latin America. What future have such people in store for them? And then there are the numerous people in our midst with hereditary diseases as well as congenital malformations (those present from birth) whose quality of life has been irrevocably impoverished when compared with their fortunate peers. Some, like victims of Down's syndrome, will never be able to live independent lives. It is known that some alcoholic subjects bear an hereditary trait. May the same not be true for some types of criminal? We certainly carry much of our destiny in our genes, but did we choose these when we were conceived?

To know all is to forgive all, runs the familiar proverb. Only God can have that all-inclusive knowledge. This is why Jesus forbids us to judge and condemn other people lest we in turn fall into judgement and condemnation (Luke 6.3-7). Some of the great mystics have sensed no judgement or condemnation in God at all - the English mystics Julian of Norwich and William Law were especially outspoken on this point, and many of the saints of Quakerism would have concurred absolutely. The limitation of the type of theology I recorded earlier on in this chapter is that it often stems from the human mind rather than from the Spirit of God, whose nature is always to have mercy. That we pay dearly for our misdemeanours is certain, and the more advantageous our position, the more shocking is the fall. This is due to the law that governs the universal order of things. The Hebrew concept of Law, as expounded by Moses, is crucially correct. If we contravene it, we suffer but, as St Paul notes, the Law is not self-fulfilling. It shows the way, but does not in itself help us to obey its precepts. Here lies the poignancy of the human situation in the world of time and space. The ultimate law is the law of cause and effect seen on a moral nature. St Paul puts it thus: 'Make no mistake about this: God is not fooled; everyone reaps what he sows' (Gal. 6.7).

Hinduism and Buddhism assert that the moral conduct in one life influences the circumstances of a later life. This is the essence of the doctrine of karma, a word which fundamentally means action. It should be noted that not all groups who accept reincarnation tie in an immediate moral consequence. The Shiite Muslims, for instance, believe that a soul passes through a succession of lives in different circumstances, in each of which he or she must strive their best for moral perfection; success or failure in this life has no effect on the condition of a later one. Ultimately, however, at the Day of Judgement, the books of the person's actions are examined, the accounts of good and bad deeds summed up, and, according to the reckoning, God assigns each person to heaven or hell for eternity. People of west Africa and north-west America see reincarnation as a basically pleasant and desirable event, not in itself related to the type of life the person has previously lived. These contrasts from the karmic doctrine of the religions of South-East Asia, noted by Ian Stevenson in his invaluable book *Children who Remember Previous Lives*, stress how much the doctrine reflects the general view of the people to life itself. The basically life-denying religions of South-East Asia have a pessimistic view of rebirth governed by the law of karma whereas the life-affirming Muslims and Africans have a much more constructive approach to reincarnation.

The problem with the doctrine of karma is its basically judgemental, moralistic attitude. It is all too easy to attribute a person's present suffering to a past-life misdemeanour and leave them to work out their karma accordingly. The grace of God, his spontaneous, unmerited gift of love and forgiveness, simply does not enter the picture at all, for everything depends on the person's own actions. This ultra-Pelagian view, that we can do it all by ourselves, is rightly rejected by Christians. Transmigration of human souls into animal bodies is also part of the karmic punishment. Without in any way despising or undervaluing our animal brethren, one has to admit that there is a power and depth to the human mind and spirit that simply does not fit in with the rudimentary brains of even our close mammalian cousins. While I have no doubt that animals have souls, it nevertheless appears that the extent of animal creativity is severely limited, and that they are incapable of experiencing the depth of emotional and spiritual life with its ecstasy and suffering that is the joy and pain of the human. I therefore see limitations to the usual karmic approach to reincarnation. It is interesting that Stevenson found little evidence of it in the cases he has investigated.

The doctrine of karma, like its approximate Christian analogy of savage retribution in the after-life for all those who fall by the wayside of conventional morality, and more especially orthodox belief, is an expression of our human desire for justice (or what we regard as justice at any one period of our very chequered religious history). Did not Abraham himself say to God in the affair of Sodom and Gomorrah, 'Should not the judge of all the earth do what is just?' (Gen. 18.25)? He had apparently cut down the divine vengeance to ten just men, but in fact God was inspiring the patriarch with a feeling of mercy. It is a good rule that the extent of our own mercy gives us a small account of the merciful nature of God. He does not prevent us punishing ourselves because of the free will he has bestowed on us, but he will come to our assistance at once as soon as we confess our fault and sincerely promise to do all we can to prevent a recurrence of our misdemeanour. The history of the children of Israel shows how short-lived this repentance tends to be; but he will never leave us in the lurch so long as we diligently seek his presence in prayer. The Christian emphasis on the forgiveness of sins, an article of the Apostles' Creed, gives us our best understanding of God. 'Jesus answered, "Have I been all this time with you, Philip, and still you do not know me? Anyone who has seen me has seen the Father"' (John 14.9). The father in the parable of the Prodigal Son exemplifies the Father Jesus reveals: he does not prevent his beloved son acting foolishly and entering a self-imposed hell, but when the young man has come to his true self and seeks readmission to the family estate, he is greeted rapturously. The final words of the loving father to his angry older son are symbolic of the joyful resurrection of the dead: 'How could we fail to celebrate this happy day? Your brother here was dead and has come back to life; he was lost and has been found' (Luke 15.32).

The love of God removes the selfishness of remorse from the sinner, and replaces it with such a love for that sinner's brothers, who are all humankind and indeed the whole creation, that he or she starts to lead a new life from that time onwards and to do everything possible to put right what had previously been done wrong. We can put it this way: Christ redeems karma, the moral law of cause and effect. We still have to work out our own salvation, and put our own house in order, but every future experience, no matter how forbidding it may appear, is now seen to be invested with new possibilities. For God is with us, and we are aware of his shepherd's staff and crook affording us comfort even when we walk through a valley of deepest darkness (Ps. 23.4). Thus the law of cause and effect becomes the law of spiritual growth into full personhood through the knowledge of the love of God.

Notes

The relevant books are:

B. S. Daley, *The Hope of the Early Church: A Handbook of Patristic Eschatology* (Cambridge University Press 1991).

J. Hick, *Death and Eternal Life* (London, Collins 1976).

J. I. Packer, *The Problem of Eternal Punishment* Orthos 10 (1990). This is a series of papers from the Fellowship of Word and Spirit, Biblical Theology for the Twenty-first Century. The Revd James I. Packer's paper is No. 10 in the series, and gives a very good account of the Conservative Evangelical teaching on hell and damnation.

ETERNAL LIFE

Long ago you laid earth's foundations,
and the heavens were your handiwork.
They will pass away, but you remain;
like clothes they will all wear out;
you will cast them off like a cloak and they will vanish.
But you are the same and your years will have no end.
The children of those who serve you will continue,
and their descendants will be established in your presence.

Psalm 102.25–8

CHAPTER 12

Growth in Time to Eternity: The Preliminaries

A mysterious quality (and quantity) that we have been presuming throughout this whole reflection is the soul, the essence of a creature, which in the human is capable of knowing God by virtue of the indwelling spirit, the highest and holiest part (using spatial metaphors), also called the 'apex of the soul' in mystical literature. The mystics would broadly agree that the Holy Spirit dwells in the human spirit (God immanent), but other, less adventurous theologians would simply see a point of connection between the soul's spirit and God's Holy Spirit. Is the soul born, or at least created, at the moment of conception, or has it existed in the spiritual world before it has 'descended' into the human psyche at the time of conception? Whatever view one takes (and orthodox 'creationism' has to grapple with the consequences of soul birth at conception just as fully as does the belief in the soul's pre-existence in this respect), it is generally accepted that the soul survives death and has some future in the after-life, even if that future is terrifying, at least in the view of some extreme Christian and Islamic theologies.

> Our birth is but a sleep and a forgetting:
>   The Soul that rises with us, our life's Star,
> Hath had elsewhere its setting,
>   And cometh from afar:
> Not in entire forgetfulness,
> And not in utter nakedness,
> But trailing clouds of glory do we come
>   From God, who is our home:

Heaven lies about us in our infancy!
Shades of the prison-house begin to close
   Upon the growing boy,
But he beholds the light, and whence it flows,
   He sees it in his joy;
The youth, who daily farther from the east
   Must travel, still is Nature's priest,
   And by the vision splendid
   Is on his way attended;
At length the man perceives it die away,
And fade into the light of common day.

The famous lines from Wordsworth's ode, 'Intimations of Immortality', describe the journey of the human soul poignantly and accurately for all who can move beyond concrete thought to deeper intuition, which is the realm of spiritual reality. The sequence described in Wordsworth's vision is very sad until we remember the purpose of our life here: to grow into full personhood, something that is achieved in the far from immaculate world of opportunity and failure, of creativeness and stagnation, of venture and cowardice, of service and selfishness, all revealing hidden parts of our own being, and in the process showing us more and more of our soul. John Keats described the world as 'the vale of Soul-making' (in a letter to George and Georgiana Keats), and this is the truth. The soul is, to be sure, present when the person is conceived, whether we take the Platonic, Wordsworthian view of its pre-existence (as did Origen) or the more orthodox creationist view of its being born at the individual's conception; but it grows through the manifold experiences of life, in the process of which its spirit should become more in evidence as it directs the person to the better, nobler way of love and virtue (the latter becomes real only in the presence of love, as many of Jesus' parables and life encounters remind us, none more forcibly than Luke

18.9-14, which we have considered repeatedly in these pages). More often the soul is tarnished by the things of the world: the seven deadly sins are good summaries. These are pride, covetousness, lust, anger, gluttony, envy and sloth – though I personally would replace anger, which is sometimes justifiable if not necessary, with hatred, a terrible emotion that is a concomitant of religious fanaticism as well as of more personal and communal matters. When we fondly think we are doing good, we are not infrequently tarnishing our soul with egoistic pride, the deadliest of all the sins inasmuch as it prevents us receiving from anyone else. Thus we exclude from our midst the life-giving power of the Holy Spirit. However, 'Pride goes before disaster, and arrogance before a fall' (Prov. 16.18), and once the consequences of that fall and the pain of that disaster have been assimilated, a new life may commence, and the remainder of the person's days may be far more spirit-directed. The near-death experience points eloquently to this sequence, no matter what views we may hold about its mechanism.

It is a spiritual paradox – and spirituality progresses by paradox until we can see the face of God in every event in our lives, terrible as some may be – that we grow by trial and frequent error. The experience of human, and indeed creaturely, solidarity, is brought home to us when we are far from home and another person, who understands our plight, helps us onwards. But this understanding would not be forthcoming had our befriender not known something similar in his or her own life. And so we are able to assist others, not by trying to do good and interfering with other people's lives but by simply being available to hear what they are saying and to listen to how the Holy Spirit is directing us inwardly. St Paul in Ephesians 4.25 enjoins us to 'have done with falsehood and speak the truth to each other, for we belong to one another as parts of one

body'. This 'membership one of another', to quote the
translation of the Authorized Version, was in this
passage applied specifically to the struggling Christian
community, but now it has a universal scope. We only
begin to know the truth of this injunction when we
have come to the truth of our situation, often made
clear by sin which strips us of the illusion of rectitude
and shows us how close we are to all those around us.
To seek self-comfort at the expense of caring for other
people, indeed to the extent of their loss, is the essence
of sin, for it denies our mutual inter-relationship and
separates us from the greater life of the community and
therefore from the presence of the Holy Spirit, who is
the Lord and giver of life. Dame Julian of Norwich was
shown that sin is behovable (a necessary part of life),
but in the end all will be well. The bridging gift is
forgiveness, which both warms and cleanses the souls
of all who are involved, the victim no less than the
agent. But it may take a long time for this unifying
principle to become installed in us all. The soul grows
by the nurture of forgiveness, and its fruit is love. This
is shown by a selfless giving of oneself to others, so
that God's will may be fulfilled in them. God's will is
that in the fullness of time we should all actualize the
divine image in which we were created as a preliminary
to coming to share in the very being of God; these two
images (and promises) form the span of the biblical
vision from Genesis 1.27 to 2 Peter 1.4.

Possibly the greatest allegory in the Bible is the
story of the Fall in Genesis 3. Though Adam and Eve
are quite comfortably ensconced in paradise, pictured
in Genesis 2.8 as an oasis in an eastern desert, they are
still not fully satisfied. They are allowed to eat the fruit
of any of the trees in the garden of Eden except the
fruit of the tree of the knowledge of good and evil; if
they do, they will certainly die. Nevertheless, Eve is
easily seduced by the serpent, a symbol of the devil yet

very importantly described as the most cunning of all the creatures the Lord God has made. She in turn misleads Adam into eating the forbidden fruit. At once their eyes are opened, and they see (and dislike) their nakedness, so that they make loincloths out of fig-leaves stitched together. When God hears of their disobedience, he curses the serpent (defining the demonic aspect of the cosmic order), and pronounces a sentence of pain and unremitting hard work on both Adam and Eve, whom he then drives out of paradise which is guarded by angels and a whirling, flashing sword, to guard the way to the tree of life. What harm had the two humans done in tasting the forbidden fruit? They had established themselves as the arbiters of what is good and what is evil, without reference to the higher knowledge and guidance of the Almighty. In other words they had unconsciously usurped the function and position of God himself. If they had subsequently tasted the fruit of the tree of life they would have lived for ever in this state of supercilious domination and been creation's tyrants.

And yet did not God know what an insuperable temptation he was placing before our two allegorical ancestors? His very interdiction had imposed an intolerable challenge that aroused the free will, until then as latent as in a very small child, and the individual spirit of his first two human children, still babes both in self-knowledge and in knowledge of the world. This 'spirit' is an aspect of the spirit of the soul by which we know God through the power of his Holy Spirit. The combined spirit is a dynamic principle, one that drives us onward and will never be satisfied until the ultimate beauty is fashioned, the ultimate truth explored, and the ultimate goodness experienced – an experience, in fact, of love, a word used as promiscuously today as ever before, but whose chastity still eludes us except in brief patches.

While only a determined literalist would consider
Adam and Eve to be our human ancestors through
whose disobedience the burden of 'original sin' (a true
enough quality in its own right) fell on subsequent
generations, there is little doubt that a tragic incompleteness afflicts the human family. This tragedy prevents
us from feeling immediately comfortable and fulfilled,
but if it is accepted and worked into our lives, a blessing
may show itself, comparable to the blessing accorded to
Jacob after his titanic wrestle with the angel of the
Lord in the middle of the night (Gen. 32.22-32). And
yet we read in the first chapter of the book of Genesis
that everything that God made was good. The usual
explanation of the subsequent fall from this general
excellence is human disobedience, but the more one
considers this, the more apparent it is that the human
species was also good, by which I mean true to itself,
which is incidentally the demand that will be made
upon us when we pass through death's portals and
enter a revealing judgement. Emerson recorded the
celebrated observation that everything that God made
has a crack in it. And I think that it is here that we see
the truth of the human, indeed the creaturely, situation.
Although everything God made was good, it had also
the seeds of improvement, inasmuch as a crack, though
impairing the perfect symmetry of an object and being
the flaw through which a complete break may occur, is
also a means of expansion and growth. In an inanimate
object like a piece of china a crack can have only a
deleterious effect, but in a living organism it can be a
stimulus to growth and adaptation. Darwin's theory of
natural selection is related to this idea, except that in
such an instance the crack is often made manifest in the
environment rather than in the organism. The type of
organism that can adapt best and most rapidly is the
one that bears the hallmarks of survival.

Certainly a self-contained excellence may produce a

feeling of complacent superiority, but one thing is certain: there is no growth until our present ease is blasted from under our feet. And I suspect that this is why it was necessary for Adam and Eve to be summarily expelled from a paradise that they neither knew nor appreciated. I have referred to Adam and Eve as allegorical characters because, on the very showing of the fourth chapter of the book of Genesis, Cain, after his terrible murder of his innocent brother Abel, is sent out by God to be a wanderer, a fugitive on the earth. Cain says that the punishment is heavier than he can bear, for as a wanderer and fugitive, he can be killed at sight by anyone. But whom can he fear if, with his two parents, he is the third inhabitant of the world? Obviously there are many more besides them, indeed the whole human race. And so when we are wise we neither dismiss the account of the Fall as a prehistoric legend nor take it as literal history. It is in fact an eternal account of the human condition, how all of us are sent away from the protection of the womb and of a loving family life (neither of which can be taken for granted, inasmuch as there is a body of opinion that attributes much subsequent psychological disturbance to maternal stress during the pregnancy affecting the disposition of the developing foetus). It is a variation on the theme of the soul's growing into the ways of the world which Wordsworth commemorated in his ode.

When we are finally cast on to the waters of the flowing world, many temptations afflict us, as they did Jesus when, after his baptism by John, he was led quite specifically by the Holy Spirit into the wilderness. It was the devil who provided the temptations, as he always does. To be tempted is part of natural spiritual growth; to fall is a misfortune, but its ultimate effects may be a greater fortune, as some of Jesus' encounters and parables from everyday life remind us (Luke 7.36–50 and 15.11–32 respectively are fine examples). We continue to fall until we can open our souls to the facts of existence, and then spiritual vision is available to us. Then we can say, with the man born blind, 'All I know is this: I was blind and now I can see' (John 9.25). We can begin to see how necessary it was for us to fall from an unconscious dwelling in God's security. Now we too can start to see, and make a determined journey back to the source, but now with ever-clearing vision. Of course, our journey is made possible by the grace of God, his unmerited, unconditional gift to us, but whereas before we were impervious, indeed unresponsive, to that presence, now we can appreciate it and furthermore bring others along with us. There is no joy that does not enclose multitudes, for we do indeed belong to one another, as parts of one body.

In this most encouraging journey back to God in conscious union there is one obstacle, the terrifyingly destructive power of evil that is never far below the surface of most people when they are thwarted, disappointed or, worst of all, simply bored. In the allegory of the Fall I suspect it was frank boredom that led Adam and Eve to disobey God's instructions and follow a devious path to amuse themselves. The essential antidote to boredom is work, which may vary from physical labour to silent prayer. But in a state of selfish absorption neither of these is readily available. In some theological and philosophical quarters the substantive existence of evil is denied: evil is simply defined as a complete absence of the good. On the other hand, there are some extreme fundamentalist groups within the Christian fold (and probably fundamentalism in other religions also) that see naked evil in the form of demonic spirits perched everywhere, waiting to pounce on their victims at any loss of faith. Some ultra-enthusiastic charismatic groups are especially aware of the menace: anyone who is at variance with them is seen to be devil-possessed. We read in 1 Peter 5.8-9,

'Be on the alert! Your enemy the devil, like a roaring
lion, prowls around looking for someone to devour.
Stand up to him, firm in your faith, and remember that
your fellow-Christians in this world are going through
the same kinds of suffering.'

The devil is the tempter, and the ultimate temptation
is despair which carries with it the will to die, if
necessary by one's own hand. Where goodness is
completely absent, where love is in absolute abeyance,
life ceases to have any meaning, except for very
unfeeling types of people who believe that sensual
stimulation and material riches alone count for anything
in human life. When goodness is absent, there will be
an ignominious scramble for the things of this world,
and everyone except the most powerful will inevitably
be driven to the wall and killed. This is a picture of a
world in which common morality, a very prosaic
presentation of goodness, is in abeyance. Apart from
the acquisitive tendencies of people in a mass and the
destructive victory of the strongest among them, we
see only the approach of evil. The absence of good
merely provides a foundation, essential as it is, for
something far more terrible. The dark, almost fanatically
destructive, tendencies in all of us that have just been
reviewed, can now come to the surface with a vengeance:
anyone whom we believe prevents us achieving what
we ought to achieve, and more particularly enjoying
the fruits of what the world calls success, will be
regarded as an enemy, on whom all our own fantasies
and inadequacies can be projected.

The victim of this destructive urge is the stranger to
the national heredity, a threat, at least in the popular
imagination, to the national well-being, because of such
varying and often mutually contradictory qualities as
religious enthusiasm or a lack of respect for God, being
too successful and prosperous for the country's good or
else being uncouth, slothful and intellectually dull,

being too withdrawn from the remainder of the
community or else being dangerously proselytizing of
some new faith or alternative lifestyle. The full course
of the twentieth century, with its grotesque toll of
unbelievable cruelty committed by highly civilized
groups on various victims, makes it easy for any
educated person to put a name and face to the various
countries involved and the individuals destroyed. To
me there is here something more than a mere absence of
good; I can sense without any question a most
devastating power of evil, intent on the complete
annihilation of any group allegedly inimical to the
leading nation. If this terrible state of affairs were to
take place, the remainder of the world standing still
until it was too late, the victorious country would then
disintegrate, the power that had accumulated blowing
the various factions at each other's throats and then to
the poles of the world's surface, until all would be
brought back to the chaos out of which order is
primarily mobilized. The story of the Tower of Babel in
Genesis 11.1-9 gives some indication of what this
separation means, but if the powers of darkness had the
final word, there would be total destruction. Wise people
now see that war has no victors, although it may still
be necessary to check an even greater evil that would
threaten the stability, if not the existence, of the world.

Is the evil, destructive quality residing in the
personality of the human race purely intrinsic to it, the
'shadow' of Jungian psychology, or is it energized and
mustered by an external force? We should take heed if
we regard seriously the quotation from St Peter's first
letter which has already been noted, and especially St
Paul's admonition in Ephesians 6.10-12: 'Finally, find
your strength in the Lord, in his mighty power. Put on
the full armour provided by God, so that you may be
able to stand firm against the stratagems of the devil.
For our struggle is not against human foes, but against

cosmic powers, against the authorities and potentates of this dark age, against the superhuman forces of evil in the heavenly realms.' Paul then prescribes a regimen of truth, integrity, peace, faith, and the acceptance of salvation and the word of God. Prayer is the constant action he emphasizes in this struggle. Indeed, without it we are as good as lost already, for God's help alone can sustain us in a battle which will destroy our life, let alone our integrity. Anyone involved in the ministry of deliverance (a less emotive word than exorcism, which involves the mere expulsion of an evil force or spirit, whereas deliverance implies the freeing of the person from this evil force and delivering him or her into God's care; I personally do likewise with the malign spirit, which also is a creature of God no matter how distorted it may be) has no doubt about St Paul's insight into the cosmic nature of evil 'spirits' that afflict our world.

In such a situation the responsibility of the individual is not bypassed or even dismissed: he or she provides the environment by loose living, meddling with psychic and even satanic matters in a state of frivolity or frank vindictiveness, or quite often simply having an open, psychic constitution that has to be guarded by a life of regular worship if the person is not to be spontaneously infested by demonic spiritual agents. In the end we all need such a life of worship, and this is a powerful reason for the existence of religions and the practice of a regular life of prayer in a gathered community whose guided approach to the Most High has been attested by the witness of its saints. We read in 1 John 4.19, 'We love because he loved us first.' I suspect that the really atrocious things people do from time to time are the product of patterns of thought and behaviour instilled in us likewise, but by the forces of darkness. Nevertheless, before we become too fainthearted or terrified, we should remember that we believe in one God, by whom all things were created. 'I make the light, I create the

darkness; author alike of wellbeing and woe, I, the
Lord, do all these things' (Isa. 45.7) is one crucial text;
another is, 'See now that I, I am He, and besides me
there is no god: I put to death and I keep alive, I inflict
wounds and I heal; there is no rescue from my grasp'
(Deut. 32.39). In our life on earth we cannot avoid close
contact with the dark forces, whom I identify with the
fallen angels. An angel is a being of light and spiritual
power. It transmits the message it receives, but lacks
independent will, discrimination or form, though it can
assume a human shape under stringent conditions. If it
is aligned to God it is a heavenly servant, and the
messages it transmits are true, but if it is aligned to the
dark, evil fallen fraternity, it is a bearer of confusion,
darkness and despair.

Who is the leader of this dark, demonic fraternity?
Tradition sees their nature fallen because their master,
whom we call Lucifer, though a favoured creature of
God, contended with his Maker for special power and
dominion. Though he (the use of the male personal
pronoun is merely a convention, for angels have no sex)
had the privilege of bearing the uncreated, inextinguish-
able light of God, he attempted to set up his own
domain without reference to the Father (the story of the
Fall on a cosmic level). When his scheme was thwarted
in the desire for creaturely supremacy, he gathered
disaffected followers around him, and their efforts were
directed at preventing any other created form from
actualizing its own potentiality and manifesting its full
integrity. All this is assuredly mythological, an account
in which spiritual truth is recorded symbolically - who,
apart from a small number of very spiritually aware
people, can describe, let alone define, the nature of an
angel? And yet, in a situation of terror, when one's very
life is at stake, one's eyes (physical and spiritual) may
be opened, like those of the man born blind who could
both see and recognize the Son of Man (John 9.38). And

then the spiritually invisible suddenly becomes visible, and the messenger activity of our own guardian angel is open to us: we receive the message and are urged to act accordingly. It seldom shows itself in a form, although, like spiritual entities generally, it is 'idio-plastic'. This means the capacity to adopt a variety of appearances, just as the psychical body of Jesus did in the various resurrection accounts in the Gospels (Luke 24.13-31, 36-51, and John 20.14-18, 19-29, are fine examples).

It should be noted that humans and angels come from a different stock, so that the one can never become the other. Lucifer can be identified with Satan, the Adversary, who challenges the piety of Job (Job 1.6-12, 2.1-7) by bringing misfortune upon him, culminating in a repulsive skin disease. Satan nevertheless is a member of the court of heaven, and was the one who successfully tempted Eve in the account of the Fall. While Job is a purely fictional character, the deeper teaching shows that the devil has an important part to play in the spiritual growth of the human: without the severe trial he placed on Job and the pain produced that drove the righteous man almost to distraction, Job would not in the end have been blessed by a direct apprehension of God's nature, far in advance of the comfortable assumptions of the Wisdom literature of that time. Whether God meant Lucifer to fall or merely used his recalcitrance to the best purpose we cannot tell, but one thing is evident: the more we fear the devil, the closer he comes to us, and the more we hate him, the greater the victory he claims. This is because our self-righteous hatred is easily deflected on to our neighbour who irritates or challenges us, and then we start to travel along the path of destruction, quite sure that the devil resides in those whom we hate, whereas in fact he takes up an ever more secure position in ourselves. The Buddha has taught that hatred never ceases by hatred, but only by love (*Dhammapada* verse 5), which Jesus affirms as he urges us to love our enemies and pray for our persecutors (Matt. 5.44-6), for only so can we be children of our heavenly Father, who causes the sun to rise on good and bad alike, and sends the rain on the innocent and the wicked.

None of this is to be taken as an invitation to permissiveness, which, if followed glibly, would lead us to as severe a degree of human degeneration as does moralistic fanaticism that destroys the springs of human growth and adventuresomeness. What does not grow, soon undergoes atrophy and then dies. This is the inevitable fate of the physical body, after a period of good service to the person in our world; but the soul, being immortal, knows no natural stagnation. It is we who can impose such a stagnation by permissiveness or fanatical zeal that shuts down the 'spring of water within us, welling up and bringing eternal life' (John 4.14). Fortunately the block is usually only temporary, for the human spirit cannot bear to be curbed in this way. Revolutionary movements in art, music, literature, science, politics and theology bear witness to the power of that spirit in exploring and inaugurating new ways. But these need not always be an improvement on the old. Only when we have the courtesy to listen to God in prayer may we know what is really good and what is evil, a precaution Adam and Eve were too busy to remember, let alone follow.

A final thought brings us back to the angels. To quote from the magnificent prologue of the Letter to the Hebrews (of unknown authorship), when God's Son had brought about purification from sins, 'he took his seat at the right hand of God's majesty on high, raised as far above the angels as the title he has inherited is superior to theirs' (Heb. 1.3-4). There then follows, in the spirit of this very Old Testament-devoted letter, a number of proof texts from the Psalms, 2 Samuel and

Deuteronomy. The last verse of Hebrews 1 says, 'Are they not all ministering spirits sent out in God's service, for the sake of those destined to receive salvation?' In fact, the stature of the human is greater than that of the angels, because God became human and dwelt among us. Our humanity dwells with Christ in the fullness of the Godhead, and our work is to follow in the way of the Proper Man and bring the whole created order along with us to the final resurrection. By contrast, the angels are merely messengers of God's will and purpose, bearers of his light, at their most expansive. It is we who, in the way of Christ, are destined to do the work.

CHAPTER 13

Growth in Time to Eternity: The Process

In a famous meditation by Shakespeare from *As You Like It* the course of human life is graphically described:

> All the world's a stage,
> And all the men and women merely players:
> They have their exits and their entrances;
> And one man in his time plays many parts,
> His acts being seven ages . . .

There then follows a wonderful portrayal of the infant becoming a whining schoolboy, who in turn grows up into a youthful lover and then a bellicose soldier. The middle years see him as a comfortably appointed judge, but then follow the leaner years of ageing with spectacles and a piping voice. The whole body has shrunk, and all is prepared for the final act:

> Last scene of all,
> That ends this strange eventful history,
> Is second childishness, and mere oblivion,
> Sans teeth, sans eyes, sans taste, sans everything.

This meditation puts us in mind of the rather sober Psalm 90:

> Seventy years is the span of our life,
> eighty if our strength holds;
> at the best they are but toil and sorrow,
> for they pass quickly and we vanish.   (Psalm 90.10)

When we consider the brevity of human life in all its fullness, we cannot help feeling rather sad. The psalmist follows his rather sober assessment with an expression of awe at God's anger, his terrifying wrath, and asks that we may know the limits of our days so that our minds may learn wisdom. I personally do not see God's wrath as anything other than God's law, which is transgressed to our punishment, but the end of the process is the acquisition of wisdom. This is the capacity to see the present circumstance, whether pleasant or unpleasant, in the context of the flow of life, and to use it for the enrichment of life, primarily our own and then, with increasing wisdom, the life of the world. A life well lived reveals the greater satisfaction in giving to others, for then we can experience the truth of Ephesians 4.25, that 'we belong to one another as parts of one body'. An experience of true corporate unity is worth anything that the world can give us as separate individuals. When we know this, we have indeed learned the wisdom craved for by the writer of Psalm 90.

While we are alive to our responsibilities here, we have indeed to make friends with the mammon of unrighteousness ('filthy lucre' or 'worldly wealth' would be more contemporary expressions) as in the fascinating parable of the Dishonest Steward (Luke 16.1-9). We are expected to use all the gifts and talents with which God has entrusted us, so that we may effect as useful an existence in this world as is commensurate with our personalities. Success is a rather individual quality; while not to be measured purely materially, it is nevertheless closely correlated with the contribution we have made to the community. It may be an external achievement involving money and power, but these are evanescent in the world's long history. Of far greater significance is the degree of enrichment of the lives of many around us through the kindness and caring that have flowed quite unconsciously from us in the little

transactions of daily existence. We often have to fail
materially before we become aware of the soul within us
that entered this incarnation 'trailing clouds of glory'
from on high. So often it seems to have been so overlaid
with the world's shabby values that its inner radiance
has been permanently tarnished and its substance made
shoddy and unrefined. But all the time it has been
learning some invaluable lessons about responsibility,
suffering, and sacrifice that were quite foreign to it at
its moment of conception. It is quite possible that this
judgement is superficial, for in the soul's depths are
areas of profound compassion that were present long
before adult life was attained.

We have already considered the soul, but it is not out
of place to recapitulate some of its properties here. It is
alternatively described as the 'true self' or the 'inner
being'; its action is the will, freed from all outer
conditioning, and its manifestation is the inner life. It
shows itself especially when decisions of moral urgency
have to be made. We made this point at the beginning
of chapter 1 when we quoted Jesus' question: 'What
does anyone gain by winning the whole world at the
cost of his life?' (Mark 8.36). This 'life' is the true self,
or soul. By contrast, the ego is the outer, concrete, form
of the personality; it is what we present to the world,
being as it were the force of our emotions and reason
behind the action of the physical body. Until the ego is
well formed we cannot perform our life's work adequately. Our intentions may be admirable, but until we
have a powerful ego drive, we will show a weak
indecisiveness that will irritate rather than assist others.
We will tend to let people down in emergencies and be a
general nuisance. I say this advisedly, because the ego
is generally given a poor press in spiritual circles. Did
not Jesus himself say, just before the text already
quoted, 'whoever wants to save his life will lose it, but
whoever loses his life for my sake and for the gospel's

will save it' (Mark 8.35)? The 'life' here referred to is the
ego-consciousness that looks for its own reward and
welfare irrespective of the needs of other people. It is
clear that there comes a time when the ego strength has
to be sacrificed in the cause of truth, whether
intellectual, aesthetic, moral or philanthropic. Then the
person is thrown to the wolves, but in dying to the old
self, the real person is born and the soul reveals itself in
its newly-found glory, no longer pristine as at the time
of birth but now experienced in the field of life.

Therefore the importance of worldly experience lies
in its contribution to the building up of the whole
personality focused on the point of the ego, so that
when the moment of trial comes it may be found worthy
of sacrifice to God. And then the soul shows itself in its
full glory. But what happens to the ego that is
sacrificed? It is taken up into the glory of the soul. In a
perfectly functioning person, of whom Jesus is the
supreme exemplar, ego and soul are always in corres-
pondence, so that the ego is the outer manifestation of
the soul. In Jesus, furthermore, the spirit, the deepest
and holiest point in the soul where God is known, has
expanded to take in the entire soul 'substance'; so
therefore the Fourth Gospel is soundly based when it
says that anyone who has seen Jesus has seen the
Father (John 14.9). Even in the lives of very prosaic
people there may be a moment of expanded consciousness when that individual is prepared to make the
supreme sacrifice, and then we can see something of
Christ in him or her also. The martyrdom of Stephen is
an example of this transfiguration (Acts 7.55-6).

It is this principle, the soul, that we believe is
destined for survival after the physical body disin-
tegrates; it is quite possibly active even when the body
seems an inert piece of living furniture, as in the trial of
senile dementia. The question arises as to the obvious
inequality of soul structure. It has long been a figure of

speech to apply the term 'an old soul' to a person, often
remarkably young in years, who seems to have an
exceptional feeling for the things of eternity. The
siblings may be quite conventional in their reactions to
the world, hedonistic and protectively self-centred; but
somehow this particular person has moved beyond
attachment to the self, and the gaze is centred only on
the divine reality. The person is naturally religious, but
soon their understanding surpasses that of the ministers
of their particular faith, and they are obliged to leave
the fold to explore new fields of truth. A not entirely
dissimilar phenomenon is the occasional genius who at
an incredibly early age outstrips their contemporaries
and teachers alike in the excellence of their performance.
The fields of music and mathematics are especially
notable areas of stupendous child prodigies. Could these
individuals have had souls, indeed one could almost
say, are they souls, with much previous experience in a
life before birth? There can, with our present knowledge, be no categorical answer, but it is possible that
childhood genius, like childhood mental defect, dyslexia,
and autism, may have a genetic background. The
criterion of a deeper significance is what the genius
ultimately attains on a higher spiritual plane. Arguably
the supreme musical genius Mozart grew in proficiency,
and his later compositions cannot fail to touch the
deepest spiritual core in any sensitive listener. Admittedly the composer's life was not an especially fine one,
but he was the medium for something so phenomenal
that the perspective of the civilized world has been
altered by his glorious music. The life histories of most
child prodigies either fade into oblivion or else record
an instrumental virtuosity that pleases or even inspires
later audiences.

In the instance of spiritual geniuses whose nature is
the 'old soul', who even in youth seem fully acquainted
with heavenly things (like Jesus conversing with the

doctors of the Law in the Temple at Jerusalem when he was only twelve years old, as recorded in Luke 2.41–52), it could be that the matter is somewhat different. I am less happy about spiritual understanding being purely a genetic factor because it is so intimately involved in spontaneous relationships with other people as well as with God. In other words, it is not a mere skill like music or mathematics but a chosen way of life. Currently there is much spoken about the 'born-again Christians'; their conversion often seems to have a strongly emotional element to it so that they tend to become judgemental against those with whom they disagree, seeing in these other people's dissent a seed of evil (usually termed 'the enemy', alias Satan). This narrow approach is found in the fundamentalist faction of the other great religious traditions also, and is by no means a specifically Christian phenomenon. The much more healthy 'once-born Christian' (of whom Jesus himself is the great example) is truly centred on God whose nature the person knows as love, not merely with the mind but with the joyful soul which radiates this knowledge through the whole personality.

Such a person is not a persecutor and is not especially frightened of evil, though, of course, being sensibly aware of its danger. This person looks for a final conversion of evil to good rather than to its dramatic destruction in bloody spiritual warfare. Needless to say, the once-born individuals are often not especially popular with the religious authorities and those who follow them in childlike obedience, but they have already learned the great lesson of loving one's enemies and praying for one's persecutors. The born-again believer often longs for martyrdom, which in fact is a tremendous ego-booster except when undergone in the right frame of mind and in an extreme situation. By contrast, the once-born individual longs only for the peace of the world. Not infrequently such a person does

die a martyr's death, sometimes at the hands of the
religious establishment; Jesus' end is a classic expo-
sition of the theme. On other occasions the person's
death is a token of love for the downtrodden and
oppressed, but hatred is not a feature of their end:
'Father, forgive them; they do not know what they are
doing' (Luke 23.34).

I believe that such a person is the best evidence we
have at present for belief in the pre-existence of the
soul, controversial as that evidence may be. The other
source of evidence is the memories of apparent past
lives that have been investigated by Professor Ian
Stevenson, and were considered in chapter 10. Personally
I am persuaded that these memories are real, and not to
be explained satisfactorily either rationally or in terms
of *psi* with the living. The only other possibility that
really resonates with me is that the child may be
obsessed by the 'unquiet spirit' of the individual whom
he or she claims to be. If this is so, the degree of
psychical contact must be extremely intimate, because
the child behaves very much as the person whom he or
she claims to have been in a past life. Such a view is,
in any case, survivalistic, the question being simply
whether the child *was* the previous person or was simply
being obsessed by that person, who after a number of
years grew tired and released its foothold. If one accepts
a reincarnational explanation for Stevenson's cases, it
might be wondered what good this period of remembrance does to the child. After several years the
memories grow dim and ultimately fade out, so that
later the growing child and adolescent ceases to
remember them (hence the importance of recording them
when they are still vivid). Stevenson found no evidence
of retributive karma in any of his cases, but in a few
there was a kinder, more aware response to the world
around them, with a realization that the person who
acts nobly is to be prized mightily in a world of unstable,

meretricious values. It is rather a shame that to make
'value judgements' is frowned on by many contemporary
psychologists and educationalists. I think that where
these undoubtedly well-meaning people (a value judgement to be sure!) go wrong, is in confusing the action
with the individual. Thus Christ forbids us to judge or
condemn others, but he, like any responsible spiritual
teacher, instructs us to assess actions by their results:

> Beware of false prophets, who come to you dressed
> up as sheep while underneath they are savage wolves.
> You will recognize them by their fruit. Can grapes be
> picked from briars, or figs from thistles? A good tree
> always yields sound fruit, and a poor tree bad fruit.
> A good tree cannot bear bad fruit, or a poor tree
> sound fruit. A tree that does not yield sound fruit is
> cut down and thrown on the fire. That is why I say
> you will recognize them by their fruit. (Matt 7.15–20)

If one applies this test to sexual ethics, for instance,
there can be no doubt that chastity is superior to
promiscuity: there is little danger of sexually-transmitted
disease and a greater tendency to self-control and
concern for the other person. But how many people
teach this to the young, and practise it as a way of life?
The answer is, only those who know it on a deeper level,
the level of the soul seeking perfection. It is in this
respect interesting that quite a number of fervent
revivalists who preach all the virtues to packed rallies
fail notoriously to adhere to various individual ones in
their private lives. Genital sex and money are Satan's
great temptations; the higher one rises, the more
clamant are these two appetites, except in those people
who know better.

And here we come to the point of previous soul
experience, whether in this world (reincarnation) or in
other spheres, as would be more consonant with
Christian dogma (I personally believe that both occur;

I will amplify this in the next chapter). 'Young souls' look for all life's pleasures, but are not very concerned about other people except in so far as they can use them for their own ends. The end of such a life is one of anonymous suffering as the body fails, and the loneliness of bereavement falls on the survivor. At first this is merely a nuisance, inasmuch as a helpmate has left the individual to get on as best as they can. In later lives the experience of tenderness grows, and bereavement is experienced as a far greater tragedy than mere worldly inconvenience. And so the person begins to learn about the joy of human relationships, not only physical and sexual but also aesthetic, intellectual and eventually moral also. The happiness of domesticity is now treasured, and with it something of hostility to anyone who may threaten one's security. Alignment with a state political system or an established religious group adds to one's sense of belonging, and in itself is not to be despised. But what about the outsider to all these comfortable activities? It is necessary for the aspiring soul to know what it feels like to be outside the fold, a source of suspicion, contempt and veiled hatred among the unfeeling majority of whom he or she was once an unthinking member. The Nazi idea of a 'master race' was a representation of this superior majority at its most pernicious; the Hebrew concept of a 'chosen people' has been far more helpful, but the Jews, like Jesus, are chosen to serve God in a special way, not to get any special reward for their service. This is a hard demand until the soul has learned the lesson of renunciation. Indeed, once this lesson has been assimilated, the soul can claim a senior status: 'I am the Lord's servant,' said Mary; 'may it be as you have said' (Luke 1.38).

In the soul's odyssey there are many experiences, including that of total helplessness in a malformed body and utter hopelessness among the starving

millions in large areas of the world. But even if the
outer circumstance is one of horror, there are vast
opportunities for the soul to grow in companionship
with other people, perhaps within a loving family or
among the masses of destitute sufferers in a situation
of starvation. Let me say at once that I am not
condoning any of this; I am simply confronting
circumstances as they are. It is the work of civilized
people to obviate all this suffering, but little can be
done without the cooperation of the people directly
involved. Those with deeper knowledge see political
corruption as strongly tied up with destitution and
starvation, but this again can be put right only when
all the people revolt against various vested interests.
And the twentieth century has shown that revolution
can replace one odious tyranny with another. As Charles
Péguy once said, the true social revolution will be moral
or else nothing. How hard for such a revolution to occur
except among people with refined characters and
noble souls!

It is evident to me that here we are the product of
variable soul culture. The more mature the soul, the
more it can understand the various conditions of human
life and the more it can become involved in them. Jesus
is our exemplar here: he had no difficulty in mixing
socially with sinners of various types, not as a preacher
of righteousness (had he behaved thus at their various
parties to which he had been invited, he would never
have been invited a second time because he would have
shown how much he looked down on them and how
much he condescended in having anything to do with
them at all), but as one who valued their company for
themselves alone. His greater concern was like a mirror
that revealed to them their fallen state, and it also
showed them the way beyond their minor hell to the
radiant heaven of God's kingdom. It is improbable that
we can often effect such close psychic union with a

variety of people, but we can at least move beyond the confines of our own ego to impart a blessing on the passing traveller.

In the end, the only aspect of a past existence that really matters is its moral lesson. This is deeply imprinted on the soul as it takes up the emotional and rational experience of the life that is about to come to an end. The golden rule, 'Always treat others as you would like them to treat you: that is the law and the prophets' (Matt. 7.12), which finds its counterpart in all the world's great spiritual traditions, is an injunction that comes to us only when we too have known the various experiences that are common to our human condition. At the beginning, even of a single life on earth, it seems much more sensible to take care of one-self and leave the remainder to take care of itself. It is the various occasions in our lives when we need another's assistance that open our eyes, physical and spiritual, to our mutual interdependence, and then we begin to see our neighbour in ourselves. This, incidentally, is the full exegesis of the second great commandment: to love our neighbour as ourselves. There is a belongingness to one another as parts of one body, to quote Ephesians 4.25 once again. The more I become fully myself, the more I include you in myself without, paradoxically, taking you over or smothering you.

The spiritual genius comes into the world at birth with this knowledge, and his or her work is to impart it to the world. The histories of Jeremiah and Jesus show how grateful the world generally is. Even such a figure as the Buddha, who was revered in his own lifetime, still awaits the deeper teaching to penetrate the lives of his followers. As Amos wrote, 'Spare me the sound of your songs; I shall not listen to the strumming of your lutes. Instead let justice flow on like a river and righteousness like a never-failing torrent' (Amos 5.23-4). Yes, indeed, ritual observances get one nowhere until one's whole heart is dedicated to God in proper living. We ourselves are the everlasting sacrifice, and may our souls and bodies be things of glory to our Creator! Once we can see the scheme of pre-existence and rebirth as a way of growth into the knowledge and love of God, we can live more diligently now, agreeing with St Paul that 'the sufferings we now endure bear no comparison with the splendour, as yet unrevealed, which is in store for us' (Rom. 8.18). The Christian will grow in the full knowledge of their Saviour, a far more glorious figure than the personality worshipped by the masses. Indeed, Christians will have to die to him before they can see who he really is.

This brings us to the final test: a naked confrontation with evil, with the dark demonic array of fallen angels whom we considered in the previous chapter. No one attains full mastery of soul structure until this contact has been made. As we noted in that chapter, the human is on a higher level of creation than the angel, who is a mere messenger of light or darkness but without independent will. I suspect that this somewhat automatic existence was a punishment for Satan's act of mutiny; now he alone has a perverted will, while those in servitude to him (humans as well as the demons, who are the angels of darkness) follow his dictates alternatively vigorously and listlessly. The angels of light are so full of the love and power of God that their will is an extension of the will of God, which again is the human condition when love floods into our hearts and we bring others to the divine source by our very presence among them, like Jesus whose work among the masses we have recently considered. The aspiring person comes in conflict with demonic forces primarily in a situation of deliverance (see chapter 12) where he or she is in control – one should not get involved in a deliverance situation unless one knows how to cope, otherwise one should call in the help of a more experienced minister. In any case all deliverance work should be done in a team of at least two people, for the danger can at times be overwhelming. The requirement is psychically sensitive people who are centred in Christ, the form of God in the world.

But much more terrible evil stems from the perverted wills of humans, who may both attract demonic forces and harness them for their own nefarious purposes; often these people are unaware of their demonic helpers, having made unconscious contact with them through their malice and desire to annihilate all opposition to their schemes. Ironically, this opposition may be quite sincerely identified as demonic by a hate-filled populace, little knowing that the demons reside in them and not in the objects of their loathing. Religious fanaticism through the ages has given the demonic fraternity much scope for activity, as with the Christian mobs pillaging the ghettos after the observance of the Good Friday liturgy in many medieval cities, the Crusaders who exterminated Jew and Muslim alike in their ill-fated attacks on the Holy Land in the Middle Ages, and the terrible persecutions visited upon Protestants by Catholics and *vice versa* after the Reformation. Certainly the Evil One who persuaded the Jews to seek the liberation of Barabbas and the crucifixion of Jesus has not since been inactive in the Church that arose in Christ's name. Nor are the Muslims any less culpable of terrible cruelty in the name of Allah. And so it goes on. In the twentieth century, religion has been obliged to take a second place to forms of extreme nationalism, which have used Christianity, Judaism and Islam as the occasion has arisen.

The supreme evil of this century has been fascism with its theories of racial superiority, which plummeted in human bestiality under the Nazism of Hitler in Germany in the 1930s and early 1940s. Here was a system that aimed at the complete annihilation of the

Jews under the most horrifying conditions: six million perished before the collapse of the Nazi state in 1945. The spirits of darkness showed themselves as demonic powers that were closely interlinked with malicious humans who were the master conspirators, as is always the case when an apparently normal person (in terms of mental disease as labelled psychiatrically) commits a terrible crime. In other words, demonic infestation is no excuse for human bestiality; at the most the demonic agents work by aggravating the human hatred, lust, or covetousness, as the case may be. What it appears to be is this, that the soul that grows has to come to terms with all conditions, not only of humans but of the world.

With these thoughts let us ponder with gratitude the life and sacrifice of a Russian Orthodox religious, Mother Maria (Elizaveta Yuryevna Skobtsova, 1891-1945). As a young woman she had combined interests in poetry, literature, politics and theology. She was a friend of Alexander Blok and a poet in her own right. She joined the Socialist Revolutionary Party, and after the revolution she became the first woman mayor in a city called Anapa. She was also the first woman to study theology as an external student at St Petersburg Academy. She made her religious profession in 1932, and devoted her great energy and rare intellectual gifts to missionary and philanthropic work. An able speaker, she was at one time a travelling secretary of the Student Christian Movement. She took a leading part in the League of Orthodox Culture, but her main allegiance was given to Orthodox Action, a society which dealt with the most hopeless cases of destitution and disintegration among the Russian exiles. Mother Maria, in her black habit, was a familiar figure in French prisons and lunatic asylums. She visited them regularly and was instrumental in helping their Russian inmates, many of whom were tragically handicapped by their lack of knowledge of French. She herself lived a life of poverty, sharing all the privations of the downtrodden and the outcasts, and thus was able to assist and uplift them. During the German occupation she was arrested in February 1943 with her son Yuri (she was married before she took the monastic vow) and her faithful collaborator Father Dmitry Klepinin. All three were accused of aiding the Jews, and all perished in the concentration camps. Mother Maria died a martyr's death in the gas chambers in April 1945, having changed places with a young Jewish mother. This account of the life of Mother Maria is taken from a lovely book by Nicolas Zernov called *The Russian Religious Renaissance of the Twentieth Century*, published in 1963. Nicolas, too, was a lovely person, fully ecumenical when the term was quite eccentric; how he must be watching with joy the liberation of Russia from his place in the blessed after-life! I trust that his prayers are with it in its struggle towards democratic freedom.

To come down to earth once more, if the soul experiences many lifetimes on this earth or elsewhere, can one speak of the integrity of the person? In other words, who am I? Here, I think the meditation by Shakespeare from *As You Like It* which opened this chapter can give us a clue. Can the soldier identify himself with the infant he once was, or the judge with the mischievous schoolboy? The old man can probably remember something of his boyhood, but his grasp of more recent events, including those when he was a soldier and a judge, becomes ever more faulty, so that people whom he met even the other day escape his memory. The senile man would be foreign to all the others. The body changes so irrevocably with age that many of our childhood friends and undergraduate colleagues would not recognize us in our elderly frames.

Change and decay in all around I see;
O Thou, who changest not, abide with me.

These verses from Henry Francis Lyte's hymn, 'Abide
with Me', give us our answer. It is God in us that does
not change. The soul assuredly ought to grow in love
and wisdom during a well-spent life, but its essence
remains, only becoming more beautiful as we live a life
of something of the radiant self-sacrifice of Mother
Maria and the numerous saints of the religions throughout the ages. Ian Stevenson, in *Children Who Remember
Previous Lives*, defines a saint as a genius of morality.
To some of us this may seem rather dry, but we should
remember that some of the Fathers of the Church have
not always attained that level. The terrible anti-Judaism
of many of the Fathers, notably St John Chrysostom,
has had baneful consequences down the ages, primarily,
of course, on the Jews, but also in a much more accusing
way on the Church. The soul of the Church is still far
from well-formed; if it were, the whole world would
resonate to Christian values as cited by Jesus himself.

We can be recognized by our soul, the inward
humanity that is renewed day by day (2 Cor. 4.16). If
we were spiritually acute we would be able to identify
the grown person from the child. Certainly we should
be able to do this in our own lives. But alas, our
attention is turned so sharply outwards that we seldom
have the opportunity of seeing ourselves as we are until
disaster strikes. We thought about this in the early
chapters of the book, especially in regard to preparing
for death.

I have little doubt that we will recognize our loved
ones on the other side of death by the structure of their
souls, which may be idioplastic if necessary, producing
a physical form commensurate with what we knew
while the person was alive with us on earth. But this
would be a temporary phase – if we can indeed use
categories of time 'on the other side'. The soul can,
moreover, straddle this world and the next. It can be
there to welcome a newly deceased person, while at the

same time being reincarnated in a young child. What I am saying is this: in the world of life, and there is only one life which is the life eternal, we are more mutable than we would have expected. When the great Protestant mystic Jakob Boehme was asked, 'Whither goeth the soul when the body dyeth?', he replied, 'There is no necessity for it to go any whither.' Death is an altered state of consciousness in which we see many things that we had previously ignored in the opacity of worldly existence.

Note
The book mentioned in the course of this chapter is:
N. Zernov, *The Russian Religious Renaissance of the Twentieth Century* (London, Darton, Longman & Todd 1963).

CHAPTER 14

Death and Eternity

Towards the end of chapter 7 I described some personal experience I myself have had in helping on the dying souls of some people I had previously been counselling. I brought them to the portal of the after-life, but was turned back to continue my work in this world. I will now continue to confide what I personally have been shown about the soul's journey after the body's death. Obviously this is a personal account, almost a confession if you like, and you must take it or leave it as it rings true or not in your intuition as well as your intellect. Even if you disagree with all I am about to recount, an airing of the matter of post-mortem existence can do no great harm.

As we noted at the end of the last chapter, what we call death is essentially a changed state of consciousness of the soul and its accompanying emotional and intellectual concomitants. These latter have been acquired during our incarnation, and eventually the lesson learned from them in relation to our life on earth is 'incorporated' in, or taken up by, the soul. But at first they almost invariably dominate the entity's (the most suitable word for the surviving form of the person) consciousness. In other words, what we are now is not very different from what we shall be soon after our transition, except that there will no longer be a dense physical body to shield us against a deeper awareness of what we really are in our emotions and intellects. Likewise our true nature will be very apparent to others in the same situation.

In people who had been of low spiritual awareness during life on earth, it is the emotional state that now dominates, and the emotions are negative in quality: fear, frustration, a sense of powerlessness in the face of enormous adversity, all of which may culminate in frank terror. Furthermore, the entity is not alone, but is part of a seething mass of formless life in a similar state of confusion. It (a pronoun preferable in this state of existence) cannot effect meaningful communication with its formless neighbours, neither is it open to any more spiritually evolved being that might help it in its plight. On the contrary, it is in the natural abode of the demonic spirits whose activities we have previously considered. I doubt whether these demonic agents purposely attack the entities with which they intermingle, but their very emanations cannot but add to the dereliction and terror of the situation. Here we have the terrible experience of hell. Many of us know something of it while yet on earth, but this is nothing compared with the terrifying isolation of the after-life, where there are no physical landmarks to act as beacons or signposts. This state can, at least theoretically, go on endlessly, but in due course (remembering that the concept of time is very much a terrestrial one, as is also that of space) the higher soul nature with its intellectual component does often break through the surrounding emotional chaos, and then the entity can be guided out of hell into an intermediate state in which the personality is re-established. Now the entity is an entire unit clothed in the spiritual body mentioned in 1 Corinthians 15.35-44. It has been shown to me that this 'body' is made up of the attitudes, opinions, and actions of the person while he or she was still alive in the flesh; another allusion to it comes in the parable of the Wedding Feast (Matt. 22.1-14), in which an invited guest without a wedding garment is turned away to hell. In other words, we make our purgatory while on earth. The person with a well-made spiritual body escapes the formlessness of hell and enters the discrete individuality of the intermediate state. I prefer this term to purgatory, because the purification is not a purposefully punishing one, and in fact our life on earth is part of this process of purification and is therefore also an aspect of purgatory. In the intermediate state, where people of good will (despite peccadilloes of various degrees of severity, for who among us is without sin?) will find themselves when they die, there is a calm, outflowing love that embraces all in its warmth. In its clear, non-judgemental radiance we cannot fail to see ourselves as we really are, and the experience can be shattering.

We are in fact the sole judge, but in the face of so much love the shame can be scarcely bearable: this is in essence the purifying aspect of the intermediate state, plane or dimension. We have in fact to let go of our pride. William Blake, in one of his lovely *Songs of Innocence* called 'The Little Black Boy' writes,

> And we are put on earth a little space,
> That we may learn to bear the beams of love.

This love is the experience of Christ that Christians rightly anticipate, but in it they will find members of other faiths also. The essential requirements are laid down in Matthew 7.21-3 and 25.31-46, an awesome, magnificent parable which I questioned in chapter 5. It is the finality of the punishment that I find intolerable, not the content of the parable. Returning to William Blake, the purgatorial exposure to love (all of which comes from God, whose nature is love) that he speaks of extends also to the after-life. Here we are able to see the truth without any outside punishment. In this state of clarified inner vision we recall the events of our earthly life, in a way pointed to in the near-death experience that leads back to an amended way of life on earth. Now we are no longer alone, but with the personalities of all those whom once we knew as incarnate beings, or persons, while we lived on earth.

We recognize each other through our spiritual bodies, but even more strongly through the essence that permeates these bodies. This essence is the soul, which becomes ever more radiant as we work through past enmities and resentments (in which we were cause or victim depending on the situation). The pivotal sentence of the Lord's Prayer - 'Forgive us our trespasses as we forgive those who trespass against us' - assumes a timeless urgency, and the more we can accept forgiveness, the less important do our own grievances become, until we are all one in God's love. We love because he loved us first (1 John 4.19). Our work in eternity, which is now as well as in the after-life, is to lift up all created things to God's love, and then indeed death will be swallowed up and victory won (1 Cor. 15.54).

This is the state of heaven described by mystics in their moments of illumination. But none of us can 'be' in it, using spatial language, until we are all in it. If love is the power that moves the universe, to compress Dante's sentence from the *Paradiso* section of *The Divine Comedy*, that love will never rest until all its creatures are within its fold. But we have to make the choice, for free will is not overridden. A comforting universalism is as inadequate as an eternal damnation in the hell of our own making. Thus, as Pascal says in his *Pensées*, Christ will be in agony until the end of the world. He longs for the release of his imprisoned brethren, and will give his very life for them, but they must choose to quit hell and enter a life of moral responsibility. The matter is one of everlasting hell versus eternal hell. The former I can accept, but cannot believe the latter, despite some of Jesus' most categorical parables on the subject (those comprising Matthew 25 and Luke 16.19-31 being the most explicit). That which is everlasting is within the time-scale and could theoretically embrace millions of years. But it is also within the scope of termination, so that a new life could begin when there was sincere penitence for past sins. By contrast, eternity is outside the time-scale; to it time cannot be added, for it is a different mode of reality. Therefore eternal hell cannot be reversed, and repentance is vain. Such a lack of forgiveness shows the divine nature in a terrible light, especially after Jesus' answer to Peter: 'Then Peter came to him and asked, "Lord, how often am I to forgive my brother if he goes on wronging me? As many as seven times?" Jesus replied, "I do not say seven times but seventy times seven"' (Matt. 18.21-2). In the parable of Dives and Lazarus (Luke 16.19-31) the gulf between the saved and unsaved cannot be traversed either way, and when Dives pleads with Abraham that Lazarus may visit his five brothers to warn them of the fate in store for them if they do not repent at once, he is simply told that the teachings of Moses and the prophets have the message of eternal life. This is true enough, but one might have expected that Dives' care about his brethren still on earth might have evoked a more positive response. After all, nobody, neither God nor the individual, profits from eternal damnation and hell or the more humane conditional immortality taught by some Christians. We mentioned this in chapter 11, in respect of survival of the personality.

It seems that Jesus was influenced by some of the intertestamental (apocryphal) literature of Judaism, such as 2 and 4 Maccabees, the Book of Wisdom (of Solomon), Ecclesiasticus, Judith, 2 Baruch, Jubilees, and the Assumption of Moses, for the imagery of Gehenna, a place of burning torment and misery symbolic of hell, as well as for the predictions of unending future torment for the ungodly. By so doing, he would appear to give them a divine authority. Personally, I give respect to the parables mentioned, but I see in them cautionary tales of what may happen if we do not amend our way of life now. If people do not receive an urgent warning of the future ahead of them both in this life and the life of the world to come, they soon drift into an easy universalism, that all will be well in the end. Thus we all need sharp jolts to keep going on, lest we become entranced with the fleshpots of material illusion. The preliminary teaching of Moses and the prophets paved the way for the work of John the Baptist (Matt. 3.1-12). Although Jesus' ministry was of a different order (Matt. 11.2-6), he too needed to sharpen the general populace with a sense of urgency, especially as the end of the present world order was believed to be imminent.

It is often suggested that more explicit teaching about hell and damnation would produce a better-directed younger generation. This may be so, but such an approach has a slightly sadistic ring to it, unless the love of God made manifest in the sacrificial death of the Son is also emphasized. Finally, we all have to discover that the good life is its own reward, because we then can enjoy a free relationship with God and our fellow creatures that is sheer heaven on earth - as well as in the life of the world to come. As we grow in grace we move beyond personal prejudices to a grasp of the love of God that will remain unsatisfied, until all his creatures have fulfilled their potentialities. It is my personal hope that all will be saved from the horrors of hell, and part of my own work is to help those in that dark plight with my prayers. Those in hell are closer to us here on earth than they are to the radiant hosts of the saints and angels. These work in the joy of the intermediate state, playing their part in bringing the gifts of the Holy Spirit to us in the relative opacity of the earth plane. It is very important to remember the dead in our prayers, and in chapter 9 I suggested that mediumistic people have a special calling in this work.

I believe that there is an ultimate hope for humans to be saved, but the intervening passage may be very

grim and full of pain. St Augustine himself, not a very
enthusiastic believer in humanity's goodness at large,
still prefixed his *Confessions* with the famous statement, '*Fecisti nos ad te et inquietum est cor nostrum,
donec requiescat in te*' (Thou hast created us for thyself,
and our heart is restless until it rests in thee). It is this
restlessness that will not leave us until we have fulfilled
ourselves in our own integrity, which is a mirror of the
divine spirit within us, evil though we may show
ourselves to the world on any one occasion. The prayer
of an unknown woman, found on a piece of wrapping
paper in Ravensbrück concentration camp speaks more
eloquently of this universal hope than anything that a
theologian can devise (or reject), because it comes from
the experience of the soul rather than the schemes of
the mind:

> O Lord, remember not only the men and women of
> good will but also those of ill will. But do not
> remember the suffering they have inflicted upon us;
> remember the fruits we brought thanks to this
> suffering, our comradeship, our loyalty, our humility,
> the courage, the generosity, the greatness of heart
> which has grown out of this; and when they come to
> judgement, let all the fruits that we have borne be
> their forgiveness.

The mystery of the atonement, that 'God was in Christ
reconciling the world to himself, no longer holding
people's misdeeds against them' (2 Cor. 5.19), finds its
practical fulfilment in this passage, yet the unknown
one who knew this was almost certainly not a Christian.
And, with a few notable exceptions, the Christian
Church in continental Europe, especially in Germany,
remained totally dumb while the Jews were exterminated! Indeed, 'Not everyone who says to me, "Lord,
Lord" will enter the kingdom of Heaven, but only those
who do the will of my heavenly Father' (Matt. 7.21).

The Christian Church has on occasion been as guilty of false association as the Jewish one was at the trial of Jesus. Yet religious assemblies are not to be renounced, for a great tradition is still capable of guiding the seeker to God by worship even when its ministers are fallible. No other than Christ could have transcended the wickedness committed in his name by his Church on many occasions in the last two thousand years. Thus Christ does indeed remain in agony until the end of the world, when we may hope that all thinking beings will have come to their senses, confessed their sins, purposed an amended life, and partaken of the unconditional love of God as portrayed in the reception home of the Prodigal Son by his overjoyed father.

What happens to those who 'inhabit' the intermediate state, and have completed the process of reconciliation with others whom they knew in this world, thereby fully assimilating their worldly experience so that the soul has grown by virtue of the emotional and intellectual understanding it has achieved? When the process is indeed finished, remembering once again that time is different here on earth from what is known in the after-life, the person is now ready for more work. There is no 'rest' as we think of the word here, but rather an ongoing process of growth made effectual in service. For this to happen, the person is sent on the way (gender is no longer a binding issue, at least as we interpret the term) into one of the many dwelling places of God's house (John 14.2). Among these is our own planet, but there are doubtless others also – hence 'rebirth' is generally a more satisfactory term than 'reincarnation' – but I have little doubt that many souls do reincarnate. This is not to be seen as a type of punishment but as an opportunity for growth and service – the two are obverse sides of the same coin, and when we know this a great load of resentment and guilt falls away from us.

I was once 'told' by a source of infinite intelligence that there are things we can do here that are not nearly so easily carried out elsewhere. This revelation came after a period of rapt prayer; I certainly was not thinking about this matter at that time. The same source 'told' me that there was no need to worry especially about young children and infants who had died, for they had done what they had been born to do, and were now in the intermediate state. What work they had done in their brief stay with us here on earth, God alone knows, but presumably the experience was important both for them and for those who had attended them, including of course their parents. Such a thought is useful for a disconsolate mourner, especially as once again this piece of knowledge was given to me in a completely neutral circumstance when my mind was occupied with other things. In this instance I had finished the early Sunday morning Communion service at my church, and having bidden the communicants farewell, had gone to the altar to collect the sacred vessels and prepare them for the later service. As I walked away from the altar I was told about the death of the young as I have recounted it.

As we noted in chapters 10 and 11, reincarnation plays no part in the orthodox scheme of the Christian faith. In view of recent developments in reincarnational research such as I have touched on in chapter 10, I feel it would be more sensible to look at the subject calmly and with that degree of objectivity that T. H. Huxley recommended to his nineteenth-century peers with regard to facts generally (sadly not those of a psychical nature), that we noted in chapter 9. To my mind the greatest argument against reincarnation is the matter of the linear view of history mentioned in chapter 11, which I personally accept against the cyclical interpretation of Hinduism and Buddhism. If we come back time after time, does history have any real meaning? I believe the model of reconciliation is the spiral staircase: we are moving gradually upwards on the scheme of perfection, the end of which is a transformed society of the type I have mentioned repeatedly in this book. The great saints are in a very 'advanced' part of the intermediate state, the realm of paradise, where Adam and Eve started their great allegorical journey to self-knowledge and a real knowledge of God; the two are really one, for the more we know about ourselves, the more we glimpse God within us, and the more we respond to that presence, the more we know ourselves in God's presence.

Paradise is not heaven; it is an atmosphere of creaturely joy on a grand scale, and it is here that the great saints of the world's traditions work, aided by the full ministry of angels. Whether the saints are given to rebirth one does not know. I have mentioned that at least some of them were not perfect in their utterances while alive in the flesh, but many were and are pure chalices of love and focuses of light. It is probable that they simply work from where they are, being sources of encouragement for all who can receive their love and guidance. Heaven is a direct experience of eternity. The great mystics of all the traditions have been enabled to know its quality for a moment in time. There is an illumination of the whole person by the indescribably brilliant uncreated light of God. All sense of separation is lost, for we are now fully one body, and yet we know ourselves fully for the first time, a paradox indeed of all paradoxes. This is the apogee of love. It can be borne by even the greatest mystic for only a short period (2 Cor. 12.2-3), and then he or she comes down to earth to put into practice what has been shown. No one, as I have said, can 'be' in heaven until we all are. It is the abode of the Holy Trinity.

Readers may understandably rub their eyes at what has been written in this chapter, if not shake their head sadly in commiseration with a writer who has been so overcome with heavenly thoughts that he has taken leave of his earthly senses, firmly resident in the brain. I would not blame such a person, indeed I always recommend a considerable degree of healthy agnosticism when any new metaphysical theory is expounded (not that anything in this book is especially novel). But I would like to end this chapter by reaffirming that I am speaking from personal experience and not from accounts that I have read in books. I seem to be a sort of spiritual traveller, not basically a medium, who gets his knowledge at first hand. Spiritual vision is what I am referring to; it is a great gift, but like all spiritual gifts, it is given for the sake of one's fellow creatures and not for one's own egoistical inflation. I personally have suffered gerviously in my contact with the dimension of hell, which has been my special work both in the ministry of deliverance and in my more personal contact in the practice of prayer. As I have already said, it seems that entities in that awful predicament are often more open to us on earth than to the glorious angelic hosts and the fellowship of saints who are our inspiration as well as messengers of God's love for all his creation, dark as well as light. It does not surprise me that I have wanted to accompany those whom I was told to escort to the after-life right through the portal. And yet I have continually been turned back. My work is clearly not yet done, lonely and desolate as it so frequently is. But I have quite a few friends who afford invaluable help, and this in itself has made my life worthwhile. One thing is plain: the strait gate and narrow way described in Matthew 7.14 (in the Authorized Version) may hold few travellers, but those of us upon it are indeed friends.

BEREAVEMENT

Blessed are the sorrowful; they shall find consolation.

Matthew 5.4

CHAPTER 15

For Those Who are Left Behind

While we may differ in our conceptions of what happens to the person who passes through death's mysterious portal, there can be no doubt about the fate of those left behind to mourn the silent passage of the loved one into the realms of eternity. To be sure we are in eternity now, but the opacity, a comforting screen, of our physical body shields us from a greater impact with that ultimate state of being. This is as it should be, for our work is to be about our Father's business here and now. The very limitation of time and space helps in the formation of our spiritual body, as we glimpsed in chapter 14, but our comfort in the often painful, sometimes terrifying, present dispensation is the constant presence of someone especially close to us, at first physically, then emotionally, and finally in the soul where the spirit of the human comes to encounter the Holy Spirit. What may start as physical relationship grows to embrace the whole person so that we are truly one in each other, and God is the seal of that union. I speak here not merely of a marriage between two people as understood in a civil or religious ceremony, but of all deep relationships, whether between parents, siblings, or friends who have come to know and love one another through the joy of what appeared a casual encounter, but what developed into a cleaving together of the whole personality. The beautiful story of David and Jonathan as recorded in the First Book of Samuel is a biblical prototype of such a relationship, occurring as it did in face of the insane jealousy of Jonathan's father King Saul, who planned to kill David.

And then the beloved departs into a realm unknown, never to return as once we knew him or her. All that is left is an aching void in the psyche, an emotional wound which pours forth the fluid of tears until the heart seems to break and all hope is consumed by futility. Shakespeare, in a memorable soliloquy of Hamlet, meditates on death, its satisfaction, its mystery, and its future in the greater life of any person,

> Who would fardels (burdens) bear,
> to grunt and sweat under a weary life,
> but that the dread of something after death,
> the undiscover'd country from whose bourn
> no traveller returns, puzzles the will,
> and makes us rather bear those ills we have,
> than fly to others that we know not of?

This agnosticism, very typical of the intellectual type of person down the ages, infects even the most devout believer when suddenly confronted with the death of a loved one. The accustomed support has been summarily removed, and the once assured certitude collapses like a house of cards. In the final parable of the Sermon on the Mount, Jesus gives us the clue towards something that may outlast the tragedies of our transient mortal life that we tend to treat as if something to be continued forever in its present form.

> So whoever hears these words of mine and acts on them is like a man who had the sense to build his house on rock. The rain came down, the floods rose, the winds blew and beat upon that house; but it did not fall, because its foundations were on rock. And whoever hears these words of mine and does not act on them is like a man who was foolish enough to build his house on sand. The rain came down, the floods rose, the winds blew and battered against that house; and it fell with a great crash. (Matt. 7.24-7)

Everything that is not of God is a false foundation in our lives, but where God is allowed to enter, even the most humble relationship outlasts the disintegration of this mortal life. The pain is not lessened – God does not make things easy for us, otherwise we would remain as dependent children who could not lend a hand to the problems around us but merely looked for help to keep us in self-centred comfort – but somehow a future of glory shines above us, encouraging us onward through the darkness to the light.

The experience of losing someone whom we loved is the basis of bereavement, the emotional pain so caused is called grief, and the process of its unfolding is called mourning. When death has finally claimed its victim, the funeral rites of passage bring the bereaved person on to a new life of personal sustenance, while also helping the soul of the deceased to become finally freed from previous earthly attachment as it accompanies the 'take-away' personages to the intermediate, or purgatorial, state where it is 'clothed' in its spiritual body, as we noted in the previous chapter. The fuss of the funeral arrangements is useful in diverting the newly bereaved person from concentrating too immediately on the magnitude of their loss, though often the state of shock precludes any logical consideration of the consequences lying ahead. I remember the second verse of Rudyard Kipling's fine poem, 'Recessional':

> The tumult and the shouting dies;
> The Captains and the Kings depart:
> Still stands Thine ancient sacrifice,
> An humble and a contrite heart.
> Lord God of Hosts, be with us yet,
> Lest we forget – lest we forget!

This poem, written in 1897, anticipated the death of the British Empire nearly sixty years later. The death of the beloved comes sooner than this, and all that are left to remember are the straggling line of mourners, and most of these also conveniently leave to carry on their own business. 'For mortals depart to their everlasting home, and the mourners go about the street' (Eccles. 12.5). In our life on earth we are terrifyingly alone, despite God's statement concerning Adam, our allegorical male ancestor: 'It is not good for the man to be alone; I shall make a partner suited to him' (Gen. 2.18). It is noteworthy that Eve is formed from Adam himself, thus simply representing a part of him. When she dies she throws the man back on himself, but even when they are together, they are reminders of human mortality and loneliness. When we lose someone dear to us, we are completely alone for no one can fully appreciate our loss, since it is so close, intimate and absolutely irreplaceable. Those who say in all kindness, 'I know what you are going through, because I too have lost someone dear to me,' do not really know what they are saying, because no one can appreciate our grief except a person of deep psychic empathy. And such a person knows the supreme secret of communication: keep quiet and support the bereaved one in ardent prayer. In other words, let God's love flow through you unimpeded by any personal response other than a glow of deep recognition. As the psalmist says in Psalm 42.7:

Deep calls to deep in the roar of your cataracts,
and all your waves, all your breakers, sweep over me.

He continues in the next verse:

By day the Lord grants his unfailing love;
by night his praise is upon my lips,
a prayer to the God of my life.

But now God has apparently deserted him, a Levite exiled from the Temple in Jerusalem, a bereavement as close to him as if he had lost a dear relative. In the final verse 11 we read,

How deep I am sunk in misery,
  groaning in my distress!
I shall wait for God; I shall yet praise him,
my deliverer, my God.

It is indeed trust in God (translated into 'the creative principle of life' for those of agnostic persuasion) that keeps the bereaved one alive, no matter how brave a face may (mistakenly) be presented to the world.

It is when the period of shock has worn off and the helpers necessarily depart to their own concerns, that the impress of grief really shows itself, and it is imperative that the mourner works bravely and honestly through its manifestations. These are essentially four in number: sorrow, anger, guilt and shame.

The first, sorrow, is fairly straightforward: where once there was a partner there remains only an empty chair before the radio or television, an empty bed where once there was comfort and physical affection, an eloquent absence on our daily rounds, walks or public appearances. It is hardly bearable to eat in a public place alone, or to go on a tour without a partner. Others may be kind to us, but we are suddenly outsiders where once we formed part of a couple amongst our friends and colleagues. Nor is there anyone with whom to discuss our mundane concerns, let alone our deeper problems, fears and hopes. Going to a concert on our own is now a tragic plight, inasmuch as much of the enjoyment derived from sharing with someone who could respond sympathetically to something of ineffable beauty in the communion of mutually held silence until the performance was over. And then came the pleasure of a quiet discussion on the way home, amid sounds of a different timbre – loud unmusical voices, urgent traffic, and then the silence near our home. It is the small things that remind us of our total loss, how the old ways can never be resumed, at least in their well-loved associations.

Anger seems more childish, but is really a revelation of what is going on deep within the psyche. We are angry with the medical carers for their negligence or disinterest, with the one who has died for leaving us so fragilely in the lurch (a widow having to get involved in financial matters or a widower having to look after himself where once there was a partner to help in the running of the home). All this, needless to say, becomes more poignant when the man is old and somewhat decrepit, and the children grown up with their own family responsibilities to shoulder. But above all there is anger against God (or providence, if one is an agnostic). How could he have let us down like this, especially if we have carried out our religious and domestic duties faithfully? As we have noted (chapter 12), anger is not simply to be dismissed as wrong. It is, on the contrary, the emotional response to injustice, and as such has been the precipitating factor in many humane social advances. It is when anger repeats itself like a gramophone record that it becomes wearying, and then counselling can be of help. But it must not be suppressed; rather it has to be endured until it is accepted as a part of our own life journey. Our understanding of justice is clearly elementary in relation to the cycles of life and death that punctuate earthly existence. This is what Job had to learn, among much else. The amalgam of sorrow and anger produces bitterness, a destructive emotion.

Guilt is a common emotion in bereavement, and requires some careful thought. It is natural to mull over the past in solitude and to see how selfish our attitude has previously been, how inconsiderate we were to the loved one whom we tended to regard as a slave to perform our wishes, without concern for his or her own feelings. And so the ejaculation 'if only' prefixes many thoughts, which assume the character of vain wishes: if only we had paid more attention to his health, shown

how much we really loved her, listened more carefully
to what the doctor advised, had not gone on that
particular holiday when the accident occurred . . . The
list is endless, and is sometimes compounded with the
guilt of surviving when so many others died in an
accident or a massacre. Unresolved guilt is common in
grief, and must be faced squarely, if necessary with a
counsellor. Closely related to guilt is regret that we had
not fully enjoyed the simple pleasures of life with the
loved one until it was too late. Quite often a mortal
disease like cancer strikes just after retirement when
lovely plans had been made for enjoying the next part
of life without the stress of daily work. If only we had
used the previous time of holidays more imaginatively,
travelled the world and seen the sights. To all this is
added the uncomfortable truth that our love was less
sincere than we thought (apart from the matter of frank
infidelity in the past). How easy it is to over-compensate
and turn the deceased partner into a minor saint! While
this is admirable up to a point, the bereaved person
should also face the truth, lest attachment to the
memory of the deceased one may prevent the formation
of any later relationship that might at least assuage the
pangs of loneliness. Many dying loved ones advise their
partner to remarry as soon as is right; surely the
departed one would want the survivor to be as happy as
possible for what remains of the life on earth.

Shame is an obscure, but very real, emotion of
bereavement. Apart from being the odd person out in a
social gathering where once we were partnered by our
spouse and therefore an unexceptional part of a greater
team of friends or colleagues, there is a deathly feeling
of isolation in our own dereliction. Expressions of
sympathy, especially in the early phase of loss, cause
us to retreat into ourselves, and indeed it can be hard to
face acquaintances expressing the formal words of
condolence and showing the usual gestures of sympathy.

Erich Fromm in his fine book *The Art of Loving* writes, 'The awareness of human separation without reunion by love is the source of shame.' It is therefore especially valuable for those who grieve to share their feelings with other people.

All these emotions are an integral part of the grieving process, and are in no way abnormal. Just as a deprivation of food or drink occasions the sensations of hunger or thirst, so the irreplaceable removal of someone whom we have loved passionately sets in motion the response of grieving. The process should be actively accepted and worked through – Freud calls it 'grief work'. Neither should it be evaded by refusing to think about the tragedy, nor suppressed with a traditional 'stiff upper lip'. If we do either, it is certain that in due course a really serious mental breakdown will occur, which could have been so easily averted by an open acknowledgement of the situation. In any one day of grief there may be rapid mood swings between a sense of devastating loss with many tears, a nagging sense of guilt, and then anger. Between these emotional outbursts there may be relative calm. There may be a sensation of sharp physical pain as well as these emotional storms. Later on, there may be a greater apathy as the forces of pain wear themselves out. During the grieving the person may perform unwise actions, such as, in a mood of complete destructiveness, getting rid of all articles that remind them of the deceased person. Sometimes, in the throes of loneliness, a brief physical relationship may be struck up with a friend, neighbour, or even an artisan called in to repair some domestic appliance. It is fortunate that many such liaisons are necessarily sterile on account of the age of the people concerned. But occasionally a pregnancy results, which may seriously complicate the situation. On occasions a bereaved person seems to lose all sense of normal proportion. Here a concerned friend can be invaluable in guiding the person through the realm of unwise actions to a greater calm for the next day. No important decisions should be made in a state of grief; with wise outside help, such matters can nearly always be postponed in sympathy and caring.

The grieving person tends to sleep badly, eat poorly, and lose weight. Help from sleeping drugs and anti-depressants is temptingly available, but is better parried, inasmuch as it can interfere with the work of grief. Such help brings comfort rather than support for what is to come. The real work lies with the person, aided if necessary by a bereavement counsellor or even a psychotherapist where the symptoms are intractable. The object of the process is to stop holding on to the deceased one in a clinging, possessive way, so that the person may be open to new encounters and the loved one left free to do what is necessary for his or her own development in the after-life.

After a period of several months to about two years, the reality of death sinks in fully, and the grieving partner is in a position to let the beloved one go. The deceased is no longer the primary focus of thought. At the same time, the tempo of life quickens, and there is a desire to fill the gap left by the departed one with present social concerns. But times of regression are frequent, especially when a particular event, usually a meaningful anniversary, or the sudden presentation of a significant symbol, disrupts the newly acquired equilibrium. Fortunately the grief is transient, but it reminds the person of the depth of their loss. Hope quietly replaces grief as a new life opens for the bereaved person; the nature of this hope may vary from a new type of social life (but in essence a continuation of the previous style of living and expectation) to a spiritual awakening of considerable magnitude.

Not all bereavement is accompanied by severe grief; apart from the unlamented departure of destructive parents and other relatives (a distressingly common situation in counselling work), people of deep spiritual awareness tend to accept death in a positive spirit, knowing inwardly that the beloved can never be separated from their deeper awareness, whatever may befall the physical body. This spirituality is of a quite different order from conventional piety or gnostic élitism, which tend to sweep the uncomfortable fact of death under a carpet of ill-digested doctrine or esoteric theory. Neither attitude will help the grieving person, alas, because words are no substitute for the deeply felt silence of love. It is the rule for adult loss (in marital union) to be fairly well healed in a period of up to two years. But loving parents will seldom ever recover in their depths from the death of a child, no matter how brave a face they may show to the world. Mothers are especially vulnerable because of the nature of child-bearing and subsequent rearing. The birth of another child may soften the loss, but it never entirely heals the pain by replacing the dead member. Even the death of a small baby is a major tragedy (what was shown me in a moment of illumination described in chapter 14 may be of help in this respect), and a miscarriage should be treated with respect and the foetus given a decent burial, especially if it was developed enough to show its sexual differentiation and facial form. The mother is closely involved on the psychic level with her offspring of all ages, and the embryo should not be dismissed lightly from our consideration.

The first major task of grief work is to accept the death of the loved one; a direct contact with the body is very helpful in dispelling inner illusions that a reversal of the situation may yet be possible. Then comes the natural response to the concrete fact of an irreversible situation, floods of tears. The value of deeply felt and expressed weeping cannot be over-emphasized; the tears should not be staunched; on the contrary, their flow should be encouraged even if they may embarrass the onlooker. Such an observer will soon enter into the spirit of the occasion if he or she is sympathetic; if there is no understanding, the person is of little significance in any case. There is a difference between the heartfelt tears of grief and the rather shallow weeping of a baby who cries in order to draw attention to its needs. Such shallow weeping in an adult is not a part of grieving but rather an attempt to elicit sympathy from the onlooker, usually for exhibitionistic purposes. Not infrequently the tears are brought forth to shame someone whom the weeper intends to punish emotionally.

As the grief work proceeds, there comes a time when new social and practical skills are acquired – the widow learning to cope with details of the income tax or the widower being more adept about the home. The people around the bereaved person, technically called the network, are the relations and friends. They play their part in listening compassionately and giving support (but without offering comfort, like the drugs already mentioned). Comfort merely maintains the *status quo*, whereas support gives the person strength for what is to come. Thus the bereaved person can act in new ways, letting go of the past and starting to enter a new phase of life.

Finally, the bereaved person's emotional energy is reinvested in new relationships and in new avenues of endeavour. It can, according to the personality of the individual, be worthwhile having a short ceremony to bid farewell to the dead loved one. A simple letter may suffice. The empty-chair technique of Gestalt therapy is another approach. It should always be stressed that the beloved will remain in the person's memory, but now as a focus of blessing and a positive encouragement for what is to be.

Some parapsychological issues were alluded to in chapter 9. It is not uncommon for the recently bereaved person to have a direct encounter with the deceased Most observers would tend to write this off as a purely morbid hallucination, but it is wiser to be circumspect, at least if the bereaved person seems fairly composed mentally and the apparition does not recur too obsessionally. Hallucinations, after all, are simply private sensory experiences without a corresponding external object, and they may on special occasions be valid for the person concerned. Needless to say, such experiences are spontaneous and should not be sought.

The question of mediumship was broached in the same chapter. Whatever views one may have about the validity of the communications produced by mediums, it is evident that seeking contact with the deceased during the period of mourning can only serve to delay the process of letting go and starting a new life (this could well apply to the loved one also). Therefore, on purely psychological grounds, without reference to the biblical prohibitions against trying to communicate with the dead listed in chapter 9, the practice is to be avoided. To be fair, though, some mediums do have a supportive effect on their clients when other people seem to be ineffective. It is the medium's personality that proves helpful, as was recorded after King Saul's visit to the woman of En-dor (1 Sam. 28.8-25). This incidentally shows how ineffective traditional religion and its ministers so often are in a bereavement crisis.

The spiritual implications of suffering in general and bereavement in particular are immense. While some well-meaning people regard suffering as useless and to be removed as soon as possible, those of us with deeper experience can, like the concentration camp victim mentioned in chapter 14, begin to see a purpose in it all. The 'young soul' will yearn for an end to it as soon as possible and a return to the happiness of the past (as the Israelites in the desert longed to return to the joys of Egyptian slavery when they were confronted with some immediate frustration!). But those who are more experienced in the ways of the world and more aware of their own failings will strive rather for a development of the historical process both in the world and in themselves. Every experience, no matter how terrible it may be, will be seen to have a significance beyond the purely personal, and a person will never be at peace until they have surmounted their own inadequacy in a vision of universal brotherhood, peace and love. The end of our bereavement is to see the features of the beloved in those of everyone we meet on the way, just as the disciples on the road to Emmaus saw the Lord in the form of a stranger (Luke 24.13-32), who showed them the path to eternal life. I can do no better than end this book with some words of Clement of Alexandria:

> Faith is a compendious knowledge of essentials, while Knowledge is a sure and firm demonstration of the things received through Faith, carrying us on to unshaken conviction and scientific certainty. There is a first kind of saving change from heathenism to Faith, a second from Faith to Knowledge; and Knowledge as it passes on into Love begins at once to establish a mutual friendship between the Knower and the Known. Perhaps he who has reached this stage is equal to the angels.

Notes

Some relevant books are:

C. M. Parkes, *Bereavement: Studies in Grief in Adult Life* (London, Tavistock 1972).

J. Tatelbaum, *The Courage to Grieve: Creative Living; Recovery and Growth through Grief* (London, Heinemann 1981). The empty-chair technique of Gestalt therapy is described in the text.

N. Leick and M. Davidsen-Neilsen, *Healing Pain: Attachment, Loss and Grief Therapy* (London, Tavistock/Routledge 1991; first published in Denmark 1987).

E. Fromm, *The Art of Loving* (New York, Harper 1956;

subsequently published in Britain 1957 and republished London, Unwin Books 1962). The quotation is on p. 14.

I. Ainsworth-Smith and P. Speck, *Letting Go: Caring for the Dying and Bereaved* (London, SPCK 1982).

C. S. Lewis, *A Grief Observed* (London, Faber 1961).

M. Israel, *Living Alone: The Inward Path to Fellowship* (London, SPCK 1982).

S. Wallbank, *The Empty Bed: Bereavement and the Loss of Love* (London, Darton, Longman & Todd 1992).

Index

More important page references are in bold.